SCOTTISH BUSES DURING DEREGULATION

KENNY BARCLAY

AMBERLEY

First published 2017

Amberley Publishing
The Hill, Stroud
Gloucestershire, GL5 4EP

www.amberley-books.com

Copyright © Kenny Barclay, 2017

The right of Kenny Barclay to be identified as
the Author of this work has been asserted in
accordance with the Copyrights, Designs and
Patents Act 1988.

ISBN 978 1 4456 6999 1 (print)
ISBN 978 1 4456 7000 3 (ebook)

British Library Cataloguing in Publication Data.
A catalogue record for this book is available from
the British Library.

Origination by Amberley Publishing.
Printed in the UK.

Introduction

On 26 October 1986, Britain's bus services were deregulated. This applied to all services operated in England, Scotland and Wales, but did not apply in Northern Ireland or London. In the run up to deregulation the Scottish Bus Group was restructured from seven companies (Central, Eastern, Fife, Midland, Northern, Highland and Western Scottish) into eleven companies along with Scottish Citylink Coaches. The new companies (Clydeside, Kelvin, Strathtay and Lowland Scottish) commenced operations on 17 June 1985 and all developed bright new liveries to set them apart from their former owners.

The council-owned companies Strathclyde PTE, Lothian Regional Transport, Grampian Regional Transport and Tayside Regional Council also made changes in preparation for deregulation. Strathclyde's Buses was formed in 1986 and acquired the Strathclyde PTE bus fleet. It was a similar story in Dundee and Aberdeen, where Tayside Buses was formed to continue the operations of Tayside Regional Council and Grampian Regional Transport Ltd was formed to continue the operation of the buses in Aberdeen. In Edinburgh the buses continued to be owned by the local Edinburgh council with a smaller share owned by Midlothian, East Lothian and West Lothian councils, a structure that continues today.

Across the country competition for passengers was fierce with existing operators suddenly facing new rival operators. Congestion and bitter battles took place in most city centres. In order to survive, the established companies along with the new operators had to work hard to win new passengers whilst at the same time try to retain their existing passengers. Bright liveries soon appeared and increasingly these were applied in bold new styles. Marketing campaigns and new vehicles both big and small soon arrived, some operating with conductors. These were definitely very interesting times and it was sometimes hard to keep up with the changes to routes, liveries and operators. Many companies quickly downsized or simply ceased trading after running out of money or running into trouble with the traffic commissioner. Dirty tactics were seen at times, with operators blocking bus stops, running just in front of other operators, flooding the streets with extra buses and even painting their vehicles to look like their competitors. Later, when privatisation of the Scottish Bus Group (SBG) began, there were yet more changes with companies starting to change owners rapidly.

The history of the companies involved in the story of deregulation are rather complex, to say the least, and apologies if I have missed any chapters of their history during these important years.

Central Scottish

Central Scottish can trace its origins back to 1926. After the SBG reorganisation in 1985, Central became the largest SBG company with 470 vehicles. Its operating area changed to focus more on the Lanarkshire area. It gained an area covering the towns of Coatbridge and Airdrie from Eastern Scottish along with a depot in Airdrie. It also lost an area to the north of the Clyde along with Gavinburn depot to the new SBG company Kelvin Scottish. The deregulation years were tough ones for Central with a lot of competition throughout its operating area, mainly from Strathclyde's Buses. A joint marketing campaign that introduced multi-journey tickets branded 'Hop On' was introduced by Central, Clydeside and Kelvin Scottish. The original depots at Airdrie, East Kilbride, Hamilton, Motherwell and Wishaw have all now closed over the years. It was planned to merge Central with Kelvin Scottish to create Kelvin Central Buses in May 1989. However, due to a long running strike in the former Central area the merger was delayed until July 1989 with the new company then having reduced operations in the Lanarkshire area. The company was sold to its employees in 1991 and later merged with Strathclyde's Buses, which in turn was sold to First Group. Finally, in 1998 Kelvin Central Buses was renamed First Glasgow (No. 2) Ltd and traded as First Glasgow.

Clydeside Scottish

Clydeside Scottish was formed in 1985 and took over the northern area of Western Scottish with depots in Largs, Greenock, Inchinnan, Johnstone, Paisley and Thornliebank. It also had a small depot in Rothesay run as a sub-depot of Greenock. It commenced operations with approximately 340 buses and quickly introduced a bright red-and-yellow livery along with some innovative marketing ideas. These included London Transport crew-operated Routemasters, 'Skipper' minibuses, Quicksilver local express coaches and 'Hop On' tickets. It even produced a children's book *Rodney the Routemaster Comes to Town*, telling the story of the first former London Routemaster RM652 joining the Clydeside fleet. A multitude of new operators sprang up in Greenock with Clydeside struggling to compete. In the Glasgow and Paisley area it also struggled to compete against Strathclyde's Buses, and Clydeside was merged back with Western Scottish in May 1989 after only four years of operations. Although the Clydeside red-and-yellow livery gave way to the Western livery, the also Clydeside name was retained on vehicles operating in the former Clydeside area. Upon privatisation of Western Scottish in 1991, it was agreed the former Clydeside operations would be sold separately as Clydeside 2000 with the employees taking a 76 per cent share and Luton & District owning the rest. Over time the company reduced operations in the Glasgow area and passed to British Bus in 1994, eventually becoming part of the Arriva group. The company was finally sold by Arriva to McGills group, who now operate almost the entire former Clydeside area. The depots at Johnstone and Inchinnan remain in use with McGills.

Eastern Scottish

After the 1985 reorganisation of the SBG, Eastern's operating area was now focused on the Edinburgh and Lothian area with the company owning 370 vehicles. The company introduced nine new services, competing against Lothian Buses in the Edinburgh area with a large fleet of Dodge/Renault minibuses and ex-South Yorkshire Van Hool-bodied Volvo Ailsas. Lothian retaliated, introducing services into traditional Eastern Scottish areas. Depots at the time were located at Bathgate, Dalkeith, Edinburgh (New Street), Livingston and Musselburgh. The company, which at the time was one of the most profitable SBG companies, was sold to its employees in September 1990 and the SMT Buses name was introduced. In October 1994 the company passed to GRT Holdings, later becoming First Bus. In time the company was merged with Lowland and Midland Bluebird, both also owned by First Bus, to create First Edinburgh. Depots at Bathgate, Dalkeith, Edinburgh and Musselburgh have now closed. However, the company does still have a depot in Livingston.

Fife Scottish

The 1985 reorganisation had no real impact on Fife with the company retaining its original operating area, depots and approximately 300 vehicles. Depots were located in Aberhill, Cowdenbeath, Dunfermline, Kirkcaldy, Newburgh and St Andrews. A depot in Glenrothes opened in 1985 but by 1992 the depot in Newburgh closed. The company experienced competition in Glenrothes, Kirkcaldy and Dunfermline and minibuses were introduced to these towns. During privatisation of the company in 1991, fierce negotiations involving the Secretary of State and company management took place to decide who would become the new owner. It was finally settled in court with Stagecoach becoming the new owner, much to the disappointment of the employee buyout team. The company remains in Stagecoach ownership today.

Highland Scottish

After the 1985 reorganisation, Highland lost Oban depot to Midland Scottish. This left Highland with a large remote operating area with depots located at Aviemore, Fort William, Nairn, Portree (Skye), Tain, Inverness, Thurso and Wick. The fleet size was recorded as just over 200 at this time. Competition was experienced in Fort William and around Inverness from Inverness Traction. Inverness Traction was formed in 1988 by a group of drivers and other staff formerly employed by Highland Scottish. By March 1989 Inverness Traction was struggling and was acquired by newly formed operator Alexanders (North East) Aberdeen, which was then acquired by Stagecoach in November 1989. This gave Stagecoach an operating company within Inverness. In 1991, when privatisation arrived, the employee management bid was rejected in favour of a joint bid from Scottish Citylink and local independent Rapson of Alness. Many of the drivers were unhappy with the choice of new owners and defected to Inverness Traction. Highland then withdrew from Inverness, closed Tain depot and in March 1993 Rapson of Alness took complete ownership of the company.

However, in October 1995 the company was split in two to form Highland Bus & Coach and Highland County Buses. Highland Bus & Coach developed a bright red livery with Highland County Buses opting for a blue, grey and red livery. Highland County Buses retained the depots in Aviemore, Fort William, Portree, Thurso and Wick, with the depot in Inverness being retained by Highland Bus & Coach. In January 1996 Highland County Buses passed to National Express group but by August 1998 had been sold again, this time to Rapson thereby reuniting the company. The company traded under the Highland County Buses name, a subsidiary of Rapson's Coaches, until May 2008 when it was announced the Rapson group including Highland County Buses was being sold to the Stagecoach group. The vehicles still carry Highland County Buses legal lettering.

Kelvin Scottish

Kelvin was another of the new SBG companies that began operating with a fleet of 380 vehicles in June 1985. It operated around the greater Glasgow area, taking the north Clyde area and Gavinburn depot from Central Scottish and the North Lanarkshire operating area from Midland Scottish. The depots gained from Midland were located in Cumbernauld, Kilsyth, Kirkintilloch, Milngavie, and Stepps. Only Cumbernauld depot remains today, now owned by Stagecoach. Kelvin was another SBG company to introduce a large fleet of ex-London Transport crew-operated Routemaster buses to compete on the streets of Glasgow. Kelvin's first livery was two-tone blue and evolved into various liveries featuring blue and yellow. Kelvin along with Central and Clydeside introduced 'Hop On' multi-journey tickets and many vehicles were fitted with the 'Hop On' robot logos. In 1987 it was reported that Kelvin made a £3 million loss, Milngavie depot closed, routes introduced at deregulation were canceled and approximately seventy vehicles were withdrawn. In July 1989 ahead of privatisation Kelvin was merged with Central Scottish to form Kelvin Central Buses. The company was first sold to its employees in 1991 but later merged with Strathclyde's Buses which in turn was sold to First Group. Kelvin Scottish ceased to operate as a stand-alone subsidiary after the merger with Central Scottish in 1989.

Lowland Scottish

Lowland Scottish began trading on 17 June 1985, taking over the former south-eastern area of Eastern Scottish. It began with just 100 vehicles, making it the smallest SBG subsidiary, and established a head office in Galashiels. The new fleet livery was a bright malachite green and yellow. Although the company only had 100 vehicles it had a large number of depots, reflecting the large sparsely populated area it served. Depots and sub-depots were located in Dunbar, North Berwick, Galashiels, Hawick, Jedburgh, Kelso and Peebles. Interestingly a depot was also located across the English border in Berwick-upon-Tweed and some services were jointly operated with Northumbria Motor Service. The company became the first to be privatised in August 1990 when it was sold to its employees. The company then adopted just 'Lowland' as the company trading name. In November 1994 the company was sold to GRT Holdings, which in turn became First Bus. Over time the company was merged with other First Bus companies Midland Bluebird and SMT to form First Edinburgh. After a reorganisation depots were gained from SMT at Dalkeith and Musselburgh. Sadly both closed over time, leaving only the Galashiels depot remaining. In March 2017 First's operations in the Borders area along with Galashiels depot was sold to West Coast Motors.

Midland Scottish

Midland can trace its origins back to 1914 when Walter Alexander purchased his first bus. The company gained and lost a few depots during the 1985 SBG reorganisation and ended up with approximately 300 vehicles. Cumbernauld, Kilsyth, Kirkintilloch, Milngavie and Stepps, all located north of Glasgow, passed to Kelvin Scottish. Depots in Crieff, Pitlochry and Perth all passed to another new SBG company, Strathtay Scottish. Midland however gained Oban depot from Highland Scottish, Linlithgow depot from Eastern and Ardrishaig and Islay depots from Western Scottish. Gaining new depots from other SBG companies resulted in new vehicle types joining the fleet like the Seddon Pennine VII, previously not found in the Midland fleet. By 1988 the company had depots in Alloa, Balfron, Bannockburn, Larbert, Linlithgow and Oban. Balfron, Bannockburn and Larbert depots are still operational today, but Alloa and Linlithgow are now closed.

The operations retained by Midland after the 1985 reorganisation have changed very little, with the company introducing few competing services. The 'M' prefix was dropped from fleet numbers in 1989 with the company trading as Midland Bluebird in 1990. Midland was one of the most profitable SBG companies and it became the second SBG company, after Lowland, to be privatised in September 1990 when ownership passed to GRT Holdings. Oban depot was later sold to its management team in 1992 and became Oban & District Buses. In 1999 Oban & District passed to West Coast Motors. Over time GRT Holdings became First Bus and Midland Bluebird was merged with other First Bus companies, Lowland and SMT to form First Edinburgh.

Northern Scottish

The 1985 reorganisation of the SBG resulted in Northern losing its Tayside depots to newly formed Strathtay Scottish. This led to Northern concentrating on the Grampian region. Main depots were located in Aberdeen, Stonehaven, Strathdon, Peterhead, Fraserburgh, Buckie, Elgin and Macduff. Head office was located in Guild Street, Aberdeen, and the company owned approximately 280 vehicles at this time. Since 1983, Northern Scottish operated services in Aberdeen jointly with Grampian Regional Transport using a green-and-cream livery with Grampian Scottish fleet names. Clearly with deregulation this arrangement could not continue and Northern introduced new services within Aberdeen competing against Grampian Regional Transport. Vehicles carried a new blue, yellow and cream livery with City Bus fleet names and interestingly dual-door vehicles were introduced, similar to the vehicles operated by Grampian Regional Transport. Grampian Regional Transport retaliated and extended some services out of Aberdeen into traditional Northern territory.

Due to the rural nature of the region Northern saw little competition elsewhere. However, in 1988 some former Northern employees set up a company by the name of Alexander's

(North East) and introduced services between Peterhead, Fraserburgh and Aberdeen, though success was short-lived and a receiver was appointed in November 1989. Stagecoach purchased the Inverness Traction operations and Grampian Transport took over the services to Peterhead and Fraserburgh. In spring 1989 Northern introduced a new cream, yellow and blue livery with Bluebird Northern fleet names. The company was never very profitable and when privatisation arrived, Stagecoach purchased the company in March 1991.

Strathtay Scottish

Strathtay was the last of the four new SBG subsidiaries that commenced operations in June 1985. It was based in Dundee with a fleet of approximately 140 vehicles and introduced a livery of French blue and marigold, later with the addition of a white band. Strathtay acquired depots in Arbroath, Blairgowrie, Dundee, Forfar and Montrose from Northern Scottish and depots in Crieff, Perth and Pitlochry from Midland Scottish. Strathtay experienced major competition in Perth and Dundee, mainly with Stagecoach. Both operators introduced crew operated ex-London Transport Routemaster vehicles into Perth with Strathtay also operating Routemasters in Dundee. Some of the Strathtay Routemasters running in Perth were painted in a red livery with cream bands and Perth City Transport fleet names. By 1993 depots in Crieff, Pitlochry and Perth had closed; Montrose depot also closed in 2010. Interestingly, Strathtay managed to remain in profit until privatisation arrived in June 1991. The new owners of the company were Yorkshire Traction Ltd. Strathtay would be the only SBG subsidiary to be sold to a non-Scottish buyer. For a while the company traded as Strathtay Buses, but in December 2005 Yorkshire Traction was purchased by Stagecoach. This acquisition meant Stagecoach now had ownership of the former Fife, Northern and Strathtay Scottish companies. All three now form part of Stagecoach East Scotland.

Western Scottish

Western Scottish can trace its origins back to 1913 with a long-established head office in Nursery Avenue, Kilmarnock. In the 1985 SBG reorganisation, Western lost the northern operating area around Glasgow, Renfrewshire and Inverclyde to newly formed Clydeside Scottish. Western's depots at Ardrishaig and Islay passed to Midland Scottish who subsequently disposed of Ardrishaig to West Coast Motors. This left Western with depots in Ayr, Girvan, Ardrossan, Cumnock, Dumfries, Kilmarnock and Stranraer and a fleet of approximately 330 vehicles. Interestingly, the company also had a registered office and depot across the border in Carlisle. In 1985 the livery changed from red and cream to black, white with two-tone grey, later modified to only one shade of grey and red bands. The company split did not last long with Clydeside merging back with Western in May 1989; at this time Clydeside vehicles began to be repainted into Western livery but retained their Clydeside fleet names. It was eventually agreed that when privatisation arrived, if the Western employees' bid for the company was accepted, the Clydeside area would be sold on to the former Clydeside employees. Due to the negotiations described above, Western was the last SBG company to be privatised, being sold to the management and employees in October 1991. The depots and vehicles in the former Clydeside area did indeed pass to the Clydeside employees, who formed a new company called Clydeside 2000.

When Western split in 1991, Western retained Rothesay but closed Largs, with Ardrossan depot following soon after. The company was sold to Stagecoach in July 1994 for a reported £6 million and shortly afterwards the vehicles started receiving Stagecoach corporate livery. Shortly after being acquired by Stagecoach the company started expanding. Arran Transport was acquired in October 1994 and in January 1995 the remaining operators of the A1 co-operative, founded in 1926, decided to sell the company to Stagecoach. Stagecoach continued to use the A1 blue-and-white livery and name until May 2010 when the last vehicles carrying the livery were replaced on trunk route 11 between Kilmarnock and Ardrossan. This brought to an end the distinctive A1 livery and name that had been a part of Ayrshire for more than eighty years. A depot was reestablished in Ardrossan at this time, not too far from location of the former Western depot. The company went on to acquire Ardrossan-based Clyde Coast Services in 1995 and in 1997 the bus operations of AA buses of Ayr. Around this time the bus operations of Shuttle Buses of Kilwinning were also purchased. By 1997 the company's head office was moved from Nursery Avenue, Kilmarnock, to the bus station at Sandgate, Ayr, with the company's name changing from Stagecoach Western Scottish to Western Buses Ltd. The company now trades as Stagecoach West Scotland.

Lothian

Lothian can trace its history all the way back to the Edinburgh Street Tramway Company formed in 1871. The first buses were operated in 1919 with the first rear-engined bus, a Leyland Atlantean, joining the fleet in 1965. After the trams were withdrawn, the company was known as Edinburgh Corporation Transport. The company was renamed Lothian Regional Transport in 1975 and renamed again in 2000 becoming Lothian Buses. Lothian Buses is the largest municipal bus company in the UK. The company is owned by the City of Edinburgh Council (91 per cent) with East Lothian, West Lothian and Midlothian councils owning the remainder. When deregulation arrived the company was operating approximately 630 vehicles from three depots, Central, Longstone and Marine. The company livery has always been madder (dark red) and cream and has been applied in different styles over the years. Lothian Buses has won many awards over the years including UK Bus Operator of the Year 2007 and Best UK Bus Company 2002 and 2003. In 2012 Lothian expanded into East Lothian, setting up a separate company – Lothian Country Buses. The vehicles wear a green-and-cream livery. The company expanded again in August 2016 with Lothian taking over former First Edinburgh depots in Musselburgh and North Berwick. Vehicles operating from these depots carry the East Coast Buses name and livery.

Stagecoach

Stagecoach commenced operations in 1980, born out of the deregulation of express coach services that year. It initially operated a service between Aberdeen and London with second-hand coaches. The company was founded by Brian Souter and his sister Ann Gloag. Stagecoach's first expansion into bus operations came in April 1986 when the company purchased McLennan of Spittalfield near Perth. After deregulation the company then introduced new services from Perth to Dundee and Pitlochry, also setting its sights on the Glasgow area. Stagecoach formed a new company 'Magicbus' for its Glasgow operations and quickly introduced new services from Glasgow to Easterhouse, East Kilbride and Castlemilk, which competed with both SBG and Strathclyde's buses services. Some Stagecoach and Magicbus services were operated with former London Transport Routemaster vehicles. The original Stagecoach company was sold in 1989 along with the Stagecoach express services to National Express, becoming Tayside Travel Services. At this time the Magicbus company was renamed Stagecoach Scotland Limited, assuming control of all of the company's Scottish bus operations. In the summer of 1989 Stagecoach introduced new services under the Perth Panther name within Perth to compete against rival SBG company Strathtay Scottish.

During the 1990s the company expanded rapidly by purchasing many of the SBG and NBC (National Bus Company) divisions being offered for sale during privatisation. Within Scotland, Stagecoach purchased Fife Scottish and Northern Scottish. The company would later also acquire what was Strathtay Scottish, Western Scottish and Highland Scottish. The deregulation and privatisation years have been good for Stagecoach. Although the company has gone on to invest in everything from airport operation to tram operation and railway rolling stock leasing companies, they have continued to dominate UK bus operations. In 2005 the current owners of Scottish Citylink, ComfortDelgro, agreed a joint venture with Stagecoach. This gave Stagecoach a 35 per cent share in the company. This attracted attention from the Competition Commission who ruled the joint venture could reduce competition, and in 2008 some Citylink routes passed to Parks of Hamilton. The company now has operations across the world and was recorded in 2015 as having almost 37,000 employees.

Strathclyde's Buses

In 1973, Strathclyde Regional Council established Greater Glasgow Passenger Transport Executive (PTE), which had a remit to coordinate all aspects of public transport in the Greater Glasgow area. At this time the PTE took over the operation of Glasgow's Corporation buses. The PTE was renamed Strathclyde PTE in 1980 and remained owned by Strathclyde Regional Council at this time. As part of the 1985 Transport Act, Strathclyde's Buses Ltd was formed in 1986 to continue the operation of the Strathclyde PTE fleet. The opening fleet size was approximately 800 vehicles and the current livery at the time, orange (known as Strathclyde red) and black first introduced in 1983, was retained. The fleet was mostly double-deck and operated from depots in Larkfield, Parkhead, Possilpark and Knightswood.

Although deregulation day was 26 October 1986, Glasgow permitted competing services to begin two months earlier in August 1986. The company experienced major competition in the Glasgow area, mostly from SBG divisions Clydeside, Central and Kelvin Scottish. Strathclyde's Buses fought back and introduced new services or extended services into areas like East Kilbride and Cumbernauld, which up till then were traditional SBG territories. Strathclyde's Buses did well during the deregulation years and by 1990 the SBG competing services had been greatly reduced with the Routemasters disappearing from the streets of Glasgow. In 1992 a serious fire at Larkfield depot destroyed over sixty vehicles and saw the company acquire a large number of new and second-hand vehicles. Many vehicles arrived on loan to the company with most receiving Strathclyde's Buses livery front and back. The company was privatised in 1993 with the employees taking ownership of the company. In 1994 Strathclyde's Buses bought Kelvin Central Buses (KCB), which was formed in July 1989 by merging SBG companies Kelvin and Central Scottish. At this time KCB was kept as a separate subsidiary. In December 1994 Stagecoach bought a 21 per cent stake in SB Holdings, which was now the parent company of Strathclyde's Buses and KCB. This move attracted the attention of the Monopolies and Mergers Commission which in due course instructed Stagecoach to divest its share of SB Holdings. Before this could take place, First Group made an offer of £110 million for SB Holdings with the sale concluded in May 1996. At this time SB Holdings operated approximately 1,300 vehicles and the sale to First Group made First the largest bus company in the UK at the time. SB Holdings was later renamed First Glasgow. The depots operated by Strathclyde's buses were extremely old and by the time they finally closed some had served Glasgow for over eighty years. The company's depots are now located at Cathcart Road (Caledonia) and Scotstoun in Glasgow, with outlying depots in Dumbarton, Hamilton and Overton. Caledonia depot was a new purpose-built depot opened in December 2014 and is currently the largest bus garage in the UK with space for 450 vehicles.

Tayside Buses

Tayside Buses has its origins in the Dundee & District Tramway Company, which began operation of horse-drawn trams in 1877. The trams ceased in 1956 and the company was renamed Dundee Corporation Transport. In May 1975 operations of buses in the Dundee area passed to Tayside

Regional Council. A new livery of light blue and white was also introduced, replacing the old predominately green livery. In 1980 'Tayway' was introduced, which consisted of coordinated services provided by Tayside, Alexanders (Northern) and British Rail along the Dundee to Monifieth coast via Broughty Ferry. Tayside Public Transport Company Ltd was formed in 1986 to continue the bus operation of Tayside Regional Council with a fleet size of 182 vehicles. The company was sold to its employees in June 1991 with each employee investing £500. In 1992 the company had no rear-engined vehicles in its fleet, opting for large numbers of front-engined Volvo Ailsas and underfloor-engined Volvo Citybuses. The company was sold to National Express group in February 1997, at which time the livery was changed to blue, red and white with Travel Dundee fleet names. In 2015 the company rebranded again, returning to a green-based livery resembling the old Dundee Corporation Transport livery with Xplore Dundee fleet names. The company still operates from its long-established East Dock Street depot near the centre of Dundee.

West Coast Motors

The company dates back to 1923 and has traditionally served the Kintyre peninsula. The legal name of the company has always been Craig of Campbeltown. During the 1985 SBG reorganisation, Midland gained Ardrishaig depot from Western Scottish and around this time West Coast Motors became a joint operator of the Scottish Citylink Glasgow to Argyll services. This joint operation lasted until May 2008 when the two companies disagreed over new contracts. The dispute lasted a few months and after new contracts were signed in September 2008, West Coast Motors once again operated Scottish Citylink services. In 1987 Midland Scottish passed its Ardrishaig depot to West Coast Motors and at the same time Midland Scottish acquired the West Coast Motors Oban operations and depot. West Coast Motors returned to Oban in 1999 when the company purchased the Oban & District Company including approximately twenty vehicles. In 2004 West Coast Motors expanded, taking over Stagecoach services in Bute and Cowal; this added depots in Rothesay and Dunoon to the company. Company livery has always been red, dark red and cream applied in a smart traditional style. The company expanded again in 2006 adding Glasgow Citybus to the group, giving them a Glasgow base. In January 2008 the company took over operation of the Citysightseeing franchise in Glasgow and in 2013 added Fairline Coaches (Glasgow) and Bowman Tours (Mull) to its growing portfolio.

In 2016 the company expanded into the east of the country with West Coast Motors acquiring Perryman's Buses in Berwick-upon-Tweed. This was followed in March 2017 with the purchase of First's operations in the Borders area along with Galashiels depot. The company was recorded as owning approximately twenty-five vehicles in 1992, which has grown to over 200 by 2017.

I hope this introduction has given you an insight into the interesting changes that took place to bus operations in Scotland during the deregulation and privatisation years. It is worth noting that now the dust has settled, the two largest bus companies in the UK can both trace their roots back to Scottish bus companies. Currently in Scotland, Stagecoach Group owns five of the former SBG companies with First Group also owning a further five. The remaining former SBG company, Clydeside, is now a part of the large independent McGills group. As for the council-owned bus companies, only Lothian remains in local authority ownership with Grampian Regional Transport and Strathclyde's Buses now part of First Group and Tayside owned by National Express Group. Deregulation was at the time intended to encourage competition. However, thirty years on it is fair to say there is little competition on the streets of Scotland with most services operated by the large dominant PLC groups.

All the photographs within this book are my own work, captured over many years with my trusty Canon AE1 camera. I hope you enjoy this small selection that I have chosen from my collection just as much as I have enjoyed compiling this volume.

C349 LVV Central Scottish C9. C9 was one of a pair of Caetano Algarve-bodied Volvo B10m-61 coaches that joined the coaching fleet second-hand. This rather unusual vehicle for the SBG (Scottish Bus Group) was new to Newton of Dingwall in 1985 and is pictured at Glasgow Buchanan bus station in Scottish Citylink livery. This vehicle along with sister C8 would often be used on Citylink services from Glasgow to Thurso. Unusually, this vehicle is not fitted with a destination display and carries larger Scottish Citylink fleet names.

MNS 10Y Central Scottish LT10. Pictured loading at East Kilbride bus station for Citylink service 982, Alexander TE-bodied Leyland Tiger LT10 also carries Scottish Citylink livery, although this time it is fitted with regular-sized fleet names. The Alexander T body was available in TS (Standard Bus), TE (Express) and TC (Coach). Central purchased many Alexander T-bodied vehicles in the 1980s to all three specifications on both Leyland Tiger and Dennis Dorchester chassis. LT10 lives on today, preserved as part of the GVVT collection in Glasgow.

C810 KHS **Central Scottish LO10.** Pictured awaiting its next duty at East Kilbride bus station, Leyland Olympian LO10 is fitted with an Alexander RL body and seventy-four dual-purpose seats. Many of the SBG companies ordered vehicles fitted with dual-purpose seats around this time, keen to introduce local express or limited stop services. Central introduced a modified livery and used the Redline name for express services. LO10 also carries 'Hop On' robot stickers. The 'Hop On' range of tickets were valid across all three SBG Companies – Central, Clydeside and Kelvin Scottish buses – in the Glasgow area and was an attempt by the SBG to compete with Strathclyde's Buses who offered their own range of tickets. Later LO10 would pass along with the rest of the batch to Kelvin Central, operating KirkieBus services.

D828 RYS **Central Scottish R28.** Many bus companies introduced minibuses to help compete for passengers after deregulation. A popular choice with many SBG companies was the Alexander AM-bodied Dodge S56 as seen here with R28. Central took two batches, R1 – R17 in 1986 followed by R18 – R31 in 1987. The first batch seated twenty-one while the second batch including R28 seated twenty-five. Most companies introduced special branding for the minibuses. Central used the Harrier name as applied to R28, which is seen operating service M4 Glasgow to Castlemilk which would be competing with Strathclyde's Buses. In the background construction of the St Enoch Centre can be seen. It was started in 1986 and the centre opened in 1989 noted for its large glass roof, which is the largest glass covered enclosure in Europe. R28 would later pass to Fife Scottish.

FNS 161T Central Scottish N19. Not a popular vehicle north of the border, N19 is a Mark 1 Leyland National in the Central fleet. Central disposed of all of its later Mark 2 Nationals to Kelvin Scottish. N19 is pictured in Glasgow Buchanan bus station awaiting its next duty, service 260 to Airdrie.

THM 679M Clydeside Scottish J19. Many people think that Routemasters were the first ex-London Transport vehicles operated by Clydeside. However Clydeside also operated fourteen DMS-style Daimler Fleetlines. They did the impossible and resold the entire batch back to London for use with Bexleybus in autumn 1987. The vehicles were all repainted into Bexleybus blue-and-cream livery before the long journey south. J19 is seen in Glasgow Buchanan bus station and has been fitted with a large non-standard destination screen which includes route number, via points and destination all on the one screen. However, it also appears to have folded over at some point. Service 36 was one of many service that operated between Glasgow and Johnstone via Paisley. Clydeside experienced competition from Strathclyde's Buses on this route and later introduced Routemasters with conductors on this route and many others.

SHS 961M Clydeside Scottish J596. Like most other SBG companies, Clydeside operated a large number of Leyland Leopards and nearly all had the common Alexander AY bodywork. However, three numbers (595–597) had Willowbrook bodies. All three joined Clydeside from the Western Scottish fleet and were originally owned by Paton of Renfrew. J596 is looking smart in her new Clydeside livery, seen on a particularly wet day at Largs bus depot.

DSD 939V Clydeside Scottish G939. Another popular single-decker in the Clydeside fleet was the Seddon Pennine VII. Most were fitted with Alexander T Type bodies but a few received Alexander Y Type bodies. Some members of the T Types received Scottish Citylink livery along with Citylink moquette as seen here on G939. Another modification to these Citylink vehicles was to move the registration plate from the bottom grill to under the windscreen. This was apparently to aid air flow from the front of the vehicle. G939 is pictured in Kilblain Street, Greenock, having arrived on service 585 from Ayr. This service still exists today operated by Stagecoach Western.

DSD 939V Clydeside Scottish R939. Another view of DSD 939V in Kilblain Street, Greenock. As can be seen, R939 has now been repainted into dual-purpose Clydeside T Type livery and allocated to Rothesay depot. She retains her Citylink moquette seats and high level number plate. Clydeside tried various different liveries for the T Type vehicles including white, yellow and red or black, yellow and red but ended up standardising on white, yellow and red. Rothesay was a sub-depot of Greenock.

NCS 117W Clydeside Scottish L417. Like many other SBG companies, Clydeside operated local express services, the majority to and from Glasgow. Clydeside used the Clydeside Quicksilver name for these services. The first livery used was a mundane all-over-silver livery with yellow-and-red flash. This was quickly changed with the addition of white making a much more attractive livery. L417 was a Volvo B10m fitted with Duple Dominant III bodywork but has had larger windows fitted. Clydeside inherited a batch of eight of these vehicles from Western Scottish, which were originally used for London work by Western. L417 is seen resting at Largs bus garage after arrival on service 597 from Glasgow to Largs via Garnock valley. Largs depot was a sub-depot of Johnstone.

B401 OSB Clydeside Scottish P401. Dennis Dorchester P401 is seen in Glasgow Anderston bus station preparing to work service 592 from Glasgow to Paisley Foxbar. She is seen wearing the later style of the Quicksilver livery, much improved with the addition of white. P401 was the first of a batch of nine Dennis Dorchester coaches delivered new to Clydeside. It featured the Plaxton Paramount 3500 bodywork. Although very comfortable vehicles, the 3500 featured a plug-style door that did result in extra time at stops. Earlier Paramount deliveries had been 3200 models on both Dennis Dorchester and Gardner-engined Leyland Tiger chassis.

C158 FDS Clydeside Scottish I158. Clydeside inherited a large number of Dennis Dominators fitted with Alexander RL bodywork after the split from Western Scottish. All were initially allocated to Greenock depot and used on local routes alongside Fleetlines. Later a batch of five Dominators G155–G159 (C155 FDS–C159 FDS) were reseated using dual-purpose seats from Alexander T-bodied Seddon Pennine vehicles and repainted into Quicksilver livery. They were reallocated to Renfrewshire depots and used on Quicksilver routes to and from Glasgow. I158 is pictured at Glasgow Buchanan bus station preparing to work service 594 from Glasgow to Gallowhill, Paisley. The original Quicksilver livery was a bit bland, but was later modified with the addition of white. I did hear from a good source at the time that Clydeside had been asked to modify the original livery as there had been complaints received of motorists being dazzled by the sun reflecting on the all-over-silver paint.

C155 FDS Western Scottish MN955. Dennis Dominator C155 FDS is seen in the later version of the Clydeside Quicksilver livery, much improved with the addition of white to the livery. It is seen at the rear of Thornliebank depot and carrying Western-style fleet numbers, a style applied after Clydeside merged back with Western Scottish.

KSD 112W Western Scottish PV912. Clydeside operated two batches of Volvo Ailsas, all with Alexander AV bodywork. The earlier batch from 1978 moved on over time to Eastern Scottish. In 1985 Western and Clydeside reseated three Volvo Ailsas (KSD 96V, KSD 110V and KSD 112V) with dual-purpose seats removed from T Type vehicles. PV912 is seen in Thornliebank depot and is beginning to look a bit past its best. The slogan on the side should read 'Welcome Aboard – We're going your way'. If you look closely you can see that although now painted in bus livery, PV912 still retains dual-purpose seating.

KSD 96W Clydeside Scottish M96. Another one of the three dual-purpose seated vehicles, M96 is seen at Glasgow Green taking part in a promotional exercise with other SBG vehicles. The livery carried by M96 in this photo was originally considered as the standard livery for the new Clydeside company. Clydeside instead went for a much brighter red-and-yellow livery.

KSD 96W Clydeside Scottish M96. A later view of M96 pictured at Largs depot on a private hire. This vehicle normally operated on service 4 between Glasgow and Ayr, a long service jointly operated by Western and Clydeside. The vehicle received a livery based on both operators' own liveries, Western's black, two-tone grey and white along with Clydeside's red and yellow.

KSD 96W Clydeside Scottish M96. A final view of M96, pictured behind Johnstone depot after experiencing fire damage on the road between Largs and Kilbirnie. For many years the scorch marks were quite noticeable on the road surface.

KSD 110W Clydeside Scottish M110. M110, the third dual-purpose Ailsa in the fleet, is seen approaching the turning circle at Paisley's RAH hospital. This vehicle was originally in the joint Western and Clydeside livery, as shown previously on M96 at Largs. Later, after the vehicle moved to service 12 which operated from Glasgow to Neilston, it received a modified version removing the Western colours, which were replaced by Clydeside red. The painters at Johnstone depot were excellent painters, but spelling? Pollok Centre is the correct spelling, not Pollock!

YCS 94T Clydeside Scottish
L684. Representing the most
popular single-deck vehicle
in the Clydeside fleet, L684
is seen freshly painted at
Johnstone depot in Clydeside
red-and-yellow livery complete
with 'Welcome aboard – We're
going your way'. The fleet name
on the side is a smaller than
normal size. Similar GCS 50V
is preserved in this livery by the
author and is part of the GVVT
collection in Glasgow.

TSJ 75S Clydeside Scottish
M675. This Leyland Leopard,
again with Alexander AY
bodywork, is seen at Mearnskirk
hospital near Glasgow.
The hospital closed in 1990
and is now a large housing
development. M675 is seen
wearing 'Best Bus with us' logos.
'Best Bus' logos were used by
many of the SBG companies,
however Clydeside preferred to
use 'Welcome aboard – We're
going your way' on its vehicles.

BSD 855T Clydeside Scottish
G931. As well as Leyland
Leopards with Alexander Y Type
bodies, Clydeside also operated
Seddon Pennine VII vehicles with
Y Type bodies; some like G931
with dual-purpose seating. G931
is seen resting at Kilblain Street
Greenock having arrived on
service 27 from Largs.

DSD 970V Clydeside Scottish G970. We have already seen that Clydeside reseated a number of vehicles with dual-purpose seats removed from Alexander T Type vehicles. This may explain why G970, seen here in Kilblain Street, Greenock, has been fitted with bus seats. It has also been repainted into normal bus livery, which although unusual looks smart on this vehicle. It was reseated in March 1988 but was withdrawn after only six months. Note also that the rear window has been replaced with a smaller single-piece window. This was a modification carried out by a number of SBG companies to the T Type vehicles.

D852 RDS Clydeside Scottish I165. As the fierce post-deregulation competition increased, many companies began to struggle. One company, Kelvin Scottish, decided to cancel an order they had placed for six Leyland Lion dual-purpose seated vehicles with Alexander RH bodywork. Clydeside ended up taking the batch. The first one, D852 RDS, was delivered to Clydeside as a D-registered vehicle still in Kelvin livery with Kelvin fleet names and is seen at Buchanan bus station about to operate service 593 from Glasgow to Erskine. The rest of the batch entered service as E-registered vehicles and received Quicksilver silver-and-white livery.

D852 RDS Clydeside Scottish I165. A later view of D852 RDS, now repainted in Clydeside Quicksilver livery. These were powerful vehicles well-liked by drivers. It was Leyland's response to Volvo's underfloor double-deck Citybus vehicle. You could always tell these vehicles had been intended for Kelvin Scottish since there were lots of blue-and-yellow fittings, wall coverings and moquette inside. I165 is pictured at Gallowhill terminus, a short distance from Paisley town centre. This vehicle, now registered D160 UGA, still existed in February 2017 part of the Swansea Bus Museum. It is recorded as last operating for Fowlers Travel of Spalding.

HSD 82V Western Scottish IR982. As well as the DMS Fleetlines, Clydeside operated Daimler and Leyland Fleetlines with both Alexander and Northern Counties bodies. IR982 is seen in the yard at Inchinnan depot and for some reason has received a set of blue-and-yellow route numbers, presumably from a similar former Kelvin vehicle. Similar HSD 73V is preserved in this livery by the author and is part of the GVVT collection in Glasgow.

XSJ 663T Clydeside Scottish M63. Northern Counties-bodied Leyland Fleetline M63 is seen in Glasgow Buchanan bus station having arrived from Newton Mearns on service 2. This was one of a few vehicles to be fitted with an early trial Flip Dot Display.

ECS 888V Western Scottish IR888. Clydeside struggled in the deregulation years and was eventually merged back with Western Scottish until privatisation when the company was again split from Western. When the companies were merged it was decided to adopt the Western black, white, grey and red livery along with Clydeside fleet names. IR888 is seen in the yard at Inchinnan depot having previously operated service 23 from Glasgow to Erskine. This was one of a number of routes that Clydeside introduced crew operated Routemasters onto post-deregulation to compete with new competition.

TYS 259W Western Scottish MN929. This Alexander RL-bodied Dennis Dominator MN929 was part of a batch of four that Clydeside acquired from Eastern Scottish, who in turn acquired them from Central Scottish. They were fitted with Rolls-Royce Eagle engines and were well known to be rather thirsty, so much so they were unable to complete a day's work without being refueled. This may explain why they never settled long with any operator! MN929 is pictured in the yard at Thornliebank depot. The depot still exists today but is now a council vehicle depot.

GSB 147Y Clydeside Scottish G147. Dennis Dominator G147 is seen picking up passengers at Kilblain Street, Greenock, in a full-advert livery for Clydeside's own 'Hop On' tickets. Volvo Ailsa J97 at Johnstone received a similar livery. G147 was one of two delivered in 1983 that were fitted with a non-standard Maxwell gearbox, the other being G146. Clydeside sold all their Dominators later to Hong Kong with the exception of the two Maxwell gearbox fitted examples. Some were known to be operating in Hong Kong fairly recently.

OMS 910W Western Scottish JO990. An unusual vehicle in the Clydeside fleet was OMS 910W. This was an ECW-bodied Leyland Olympian that started life as a demonstrator. Before joining the Clydeside fleet she also operated with Midland and Northern Scottish. JO990 later joined the Stagecoach fleet based at Perth. JO990 is seen in the square at Johnstone, freshly repainted in Clydeside livery. However, it is missing the Scottish part of the fleet name. Service 30 was the local Johnstone service and normally the preserve of the Dodge S56 Skipper-branded minibuses.

D304 SDS Clydeside Scottish J304. Like many other operators, Clydeside ordered a large number of minibuses to help fight off competition. Clydeside opted for the Dodge S56 with Alexander AM bodywork. Clydeside used the Skipper name for the minibuses and the second batch even received Skipper-branded moquette on the seats. Representing the first batch (301–322), J304 is seen at Largs bus depot while operating service 28 the Largs Local service.

D300 SDS Clydeside Scottish P322. Two members from each batch received dual-purpose seating from new. D300 SDS also received fleet number P322 rather than P300. It is seen at the turning circle at Paisley RAH hospital while operating Paisley local service 60.

E355 WYS Clydeside Scottish P355. The second batch of minibuses also contained two dual-purpose seated vehicles (354 and 355). This time the dual-purpose vehicles received Quicksilver livery. P355 is seen in Morar Drive, Paisley, operating a mundane service 58 to Renfrew Ferry.

E341 WYS Clydeside Scottish G341. The second batch of minibuses were badged as Renault vehicles and received Skipper-branded moquette. G341 is seen on lay over near Kilblain Street, Greenock, having worked service 51 to Pennyfern. Greenock became a hot bed of competition during the deregulation years. Many new operators sprang up and fought hard against Clydeside, who for many years struggled to survive in the Greenock area. The building in the background is a new supermarket being constructed for William Low, which became Tesco and is now a B&M store.

E354 WYS Western Scottish PD354. The other dual-purpose seated vehicle, PD354, is seen wearing Western livery with Clydeside fleet names in the yard at Johnstone depot. I always felt this livery suited these vehicles very well.

SUS 265 W Clydeside Scottish L365. Seen here on a foggy morning in the yard at Johnstone depot is L365, an Alexander S-bodied Ford A0609 minibus. This odd looking vehicle started life with Central Scottish. It passed to Clydeside and it was intended for use on the Largs local service before moving on quickly to Strathtay Scottish. I never experienced a run on this vehicle but understand it was not the most reliable.

WLT 652 Clydeside Scottish RM652. Clydeside operated over seventy former London Transport Routemaster buses. They were deployed on routes that experienced competition from other operators including Strathclyde's Buses, where it was felt the addition of a conductor would help Clydeside compete. Most operated from Glasgow to Paisley, Renfrew, Erskine and the south side of Glasgow. They were based at Johnstone, Paisley, Inchinnan and Thornliebank depots. RM652 was the first to arrive and was exhibited at an open day event at Paisley garage before being trialed on various routes. Later Clydeside applied names to each Routemaster, all beginning with the letter 'R'. RM652 became *Rodney the Routemaster* and a children's book was produced by Clydeside. RM652 is seen in Johnstone depot yard fresh from the paint shop. The author had a summer job working at Johnstone depot during this time and completed some of the interior painting on *Rodney*. RM652 is still in regular service today and can be found operating on heritage service 15 in London, restored back to LT red livery. The lower deck still has a Clydeside poster fitted on the front bulkhead commemorating its time north of the border.

WLT 416 Clydeside Scottish RM416. RM416 received a special livery for Aberlour Charity, which comprised half Clydeside and half London Transport livery. RM416 is pictured at Summerston terminus. Behind can be seen a Clydeside Scottish Leyland Leopard and Strathclyde's Buses Leyland Atlantean.

WLT 900 Clydeside Scottish RML900. RML900 was the first RML to operate outside of London. It was sold to Clydeside in a damaged condition for spare parts. However, Clydeside spent four months rebuilding the vehicle. It entered service at Johnstone depot alongside other Routemasters in the fleet and carried an all-over advert for *The Sunday Post*. RML 900 is seen getting ready to leave Johnstone depot to enter service on service 39 to Glasgow.

LDS 161A Western Scottish RM652. All good things must come to an end. A later shot of RM652, by now relegated to the training fleet and looking rather shabby. By this time RM652 has lost its WLT 652 plate and carries Western fleet number PC47 along with L Plates. His name *Rodney the Routemaster* is still displayed next to the entrance door.

KGJ 614D Western Scottish SRMA1. The other special Routemaster in the Clydeside fleet was SRMA1. Former London Transport RMA16 was acquired by Clydeside in early 1988 and after use as a staff shuttle vehicle SRMA1 received Quicksilver livery, fifty-five coach seats and was even fitted with small table lamps. SRMA1 is seen in the yard at Thornliebank depot taking part in the RM farewell event to mark the end of Routemaster operation by Clydeside.

B145 GSC Eastern Scottish CLL145. Alexander's developed a coach version of its popular R Type vehicle. Only four vehicles were built, two on the Leyland Olympian chassis (RDC) and two on the Volvo Citybus chassis (RVC). The two RDC vehicles entered service with Eastern and wore Citylink livery. CLL145 is pictured uplifting passengers at Kilblain Street, Greenock, while working Citylink service 500 to Edinburgh. It is a pity more of these modern looking vehicles were not ordered at the time.

BGG 260S SMT Buses VV50. This Volvo Ailsa started life with Central Scottish as AH10, moving to Eastern in 1988. It is pictured heading west on Edinburgh's mighty Princes Street, which at one time was the shopping capital of Edinburgh. If any one photo could sum up deregulation in Scotland this would be it. Here we see a long line of buses in various liveries working for different operators with a couple struggling to cross the busy road.

HSF 77X Eastern Scottish VV77. Later Mk III versions of the Volvo Ailsa received the squarer Alexander RV bodywork. VV77 is pictured in the St Andrews Square bus station, Edinburgh.

LWB 373P Eastern Scottish VV23. As well as Alexander-bodied Volvo Ailsas, Eastern bought twenty-five former South Yorkshire vehicles in 1987, fitted with unusual Van Hool-McArdle bodywork. When introduced these vehicles wore a revised livery with more areas of cream. VV23 is pictured operating a service to Oxgangs.

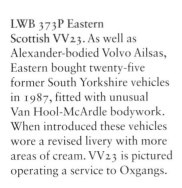

D420 ASF Eastern Scottish MR420. Eastern introduced minibuses into Edinburgh to try to compete and win passengers from Lothian Transport after deregulation. The first batch of thirty vehicles were Dodge S56s with Alexander AM bodywork – a popular choice for SBG companies. The City Sprinter name was used with route number C5. MR420 is pictured out of service in Edinburgh St Andrews Square bus station.

E437 JSG Eastern Scottish MR437. A second batch of forty minibuses arrived in 1987. Again they featured Alexander AM bodywork, but were technically Renault S56 chassis. The final six vehicles (ZMR465–ZMR470) were fitted with dual-purpose seating. MR437 is pictured again out of service in Edinburgh St Andrews Square bus station. MR437 was later recorded working for Highland Scottish in Fort William in full Eastern Scottish City Sprinter livery.

H472 OSG SMT Buses MR472. For the next batch of minibuses, Eastern ordered Reeve Burgess Beaver bodywork seating thirty-one on the Renault S75 chassis. Most wore the City Sprinter livery. However, MR472 is pictured at Bathgate wearing Bathgate Bairn livery. Bairn is a Scottish word for child.

K517 BSX SMT Buses MO517. For
the final batch of minibuses, Eastern
opted for Optare MetroRiders
with twenty-five-seat bodywork.
MO517 is pictured wearing SMT
livery at SVBM Whitburn museum
during an open day. SVBM later
relocated to Fife and occupies a large
site at Lathalmond just north of
Dunfermline. The author owns two
preserved vehicles that are kept at
Lathalmond in the SVBM collection.
The SMT diamond logo was
introduced after privatisation.

C181 VSF SMT Buses ZLL181.
Eastern ordered a batch of thirteen
underfloor Leyland Lion vehicles
fitted with Alexander RH bodywork
and these were the first Leyland
Lions to enter service in the UK.
The underfloor engines meant
the vehicles were taller than other
double-deck vehicles but could
seat eighty-six. All were fitted with
dual-purpose seating. ZLL181 is
pictured at Perth bus station ready
to work back to Edinburgh on
service 557.

OSG 61V Eastern Scottish DD61.
Eastern choose ECW bodywork
for its large fleet of Daimler and
Leyland Fleetlines. Two Leyland
examples including DD61 are
seen on layover at Edinburgh's St
Andrews Square bus station. There
is still a bus station located here
today, however the original bus
station closed in 2000 and the site
was then redeveloped with a modern
shopping complex. The new bus
station finally reopened in 2003.

ULS 102X SMT Buses ZLL102. Eastern took delivery of sixteen Leyland Olympians fitted with ECW bodywork in 1982. Four of the batch (ZLL101–ZLL104) later received coach seating and were repainted in Eastern Coach-style livery. ZLL102 is pictured passing through Bathgate on service 280. The paper labels in the window show the bus's destination is Livingston via Armadale.

SSX 621V SMT Buses S621. The Seddon Pennine VII was the single-deck chassis of choice for Eastern. Most received Alexander AYS bodies as seen on S621. The AYS body code denotes the vehicle is fitted with short bay windows. S621 is seen about to load for service 106 in Edinburgh's St Andrews Square bus station and carries SMT diamond logos. The sticker in the near side front window reads 'We also welcome city passengers' and is an attempt to win local passengers from Lothian Transport services within Edinburgh city.

GSX 896T Eastern Scottish ZS896. Eastern also took Seddon Pennine VII vehicles with Alexander T bodies. ZS896 is pictured in Edinburgh's St Andrews Square bus station and is seen wearing an unusual version of fleet livery with the addition of a dark and light green band stepped up towards the rear.

UFS 874R & OSC 61V Fife Scottish 884 and 861. Fife operated a fleet of over sixty Volvo Ailsas. Most were fitted with Alexander AV bodywork. Two examples of the fleet, 884 and 861, are pictured in the yard at Glenrothes depot. The vehicle on the left is a Mark I Ailsa whereas the vehicle on the right is a Mark 2, both fitted with Alexander AV bodywork. The higher windscreen and driving position on the Mark 2 can clearly be seen in this photo.

LSX 10P Fife Scottish 810. The SBG companies often swapped vehicles between fleets. LSX 10P started life with Fife in 1975. In 1980 she moved to Highland Scottish and was based at Thurso depot before returning back to Fife in 1990. This photograph shows LSX 10P entering Kirkcaldy bus station, still wearing Highland Scottish livery. Although her fleet name has been changed to Fife Scottish, the Highland Scottish Eagle Garter is still visible above the door.

B181 FFS Fife Scottish 981. As well as Volvo Ailsa vehicles, Fife operated a large batch of Volvo Citybus vehicles. All bar two received Alexander RV bodywork. The Volvo Citybus was an underfloor engine chassis based on the Volvo B10 coach chassis. It attracted modest orders with many operators choosing to fit Alexander bodywork with dual-purpose seats for use on local express services. The Volvo Citybus was a pleasure to drive and was competition for Leyland's own underfloor double-deck vehicle, the Leyland Lion.

C794 USG Fife Scottish 914. Some members of the fleet received dual-purpose seating for use on express services. Fife Coastliner-liveried 914 was one such vehicle and is seen loading in Edinburgh's St Andrews Square bus station. This vehicle was also fitted with a board over the top of the radiator grill advertising the Coastliner service. After leaving Edinburgh the service would use the Forth Road Bridge to reach Fife.

B175 FFS Fife Scottish FRA75. Fife opted for Alexander RV bodies for all of their Citybus fleet with the exception of two vehicles. The remaining two vehicles were fitted with Alexander's rare RVC bodywork. Only four examples of this bodywork were ever produced; two on Volvo Citybus chassis and two with Leyland Olympian chassis. Fife operated the two Volvo examples for a number of years, initially in Scottish Citylink livery then Fife coach livery before passing them on to Western Scottish. FRA75 is pictured wearing Fife coach livery and is seen upon arrival at Glasgow Buchanan bus station. Around this time the concrete surface of the bus station was being replaced, which resulted in a shortage of available operating space and vehicles parked up in odd locations as seen with FRA75.

E909 KSG Fife Scottish 909. Later versions of the Alexander RV body on the Volvo Citybus chassis received a revised more stylish front end with a less pronounced radiator grill. 909 was one of two Volvo Citybus vehicles originally built for Western Scottish. They both joined the Fife fleet in 1987 with Western Scottish taking both of the Volvo Citybus vehicles fitted with the rare RVC bodywork (B175 FFS and B176 FFS). E909 KSG is seen on layover at Glasgow Buchanan bus station prior to departing on service X26 back to Glenrothes in Fife. Similar vehicle Eastern Scottish E187 HSF is preserved by the author and is part of the SVBM collection in Fife.

B211 FFS Fife Scottish 511. In 1985 Fife ordered a batch of five Leyland Tigers fitted with the new Alexander T body. This small batch featured the TC (Coach) version of the bodywork. 511 is pictured wearing a revised version of the fleet livery with the addition of a grey band and larger fleet names without the Scottish Saltire logo. She is pictured at the rear of Glasgow's Buchanan bus station after arrival on an express service from Fife.

YSX 930W Fife Scottish 330. Fife operated a small fleet of twenty-eight Leyland Nationals including both Mark I and Mark II varieties. 330 is pictured at Cowdenbeath depot and has been fitted with large fleet names and 'Best Bus in the Kingdom' SBG advertising logos. Fife was the only SBG company permitted to use the 'Best Bus in the Kingdom' slogan.

D517 DSX Fife Scottish 417. Fife operated a batch of eight Leyland Tigers fitted with sixty-one-seat Alexander P Type bodywork. This style of bodywork was not to everyone's taste; indeed in this view of 417 seen at Edinburgh's St Andrews Square bus station, a vehicle fitted with the much smarter Belfast-built Alexander Q bodywork can be seen behind. Ownership of Fife passed to Stagecoach in 1991 and 417 has already been repainted into its new owner's livery.

GSU 341 Fife Scottish 514. GSU 341 (VTY 130Y) was a 1983 Leyland Tiger fitted with Duple Laser bodywork. It began life owned by Leyland and hired to Northern General. It joined the Fife fleet in 1984. It is seen in Edinburgh's St Andrews Square bus station repainted in a version of Stagecoach stripes livery featuring a non-standard version of the Fife Scottish fleet name.

D896 DSF Fife Scottish 6. The first batch of twenty minibuses to join the Fife fleet were Dodge or Renault S56 vehicles fitted with Alexander AM bodywork. The first eight were badged as Dodge and the rest as Renaults. Like other SBG companies Fife opted for two (14 and 15) with dual-purpose seats. Fife used the Buzzbus fleet name for its minibuses.

F60 RFS Fife Scottish 60. The next batch of minibuses to join the Fife fleet were twenty MCW MetroRiders, again some with dual-purpose seats (67–70). 60 is pictured in Buzzbus livery outside Kirkcaldy depot.

G23 CSG Fife Scottish 23. Fife ordered four Renault S56 minibuses in 1989 fitted with Reeve Burgess Beaver B25 bodywork. 23 is pictured with other members of the Buzzbus fleet at Dunfermline depot. Deregulation competition was felt by Fife in Glenrothes, Kirkcaldy and Dunfermline.

1983 NT Highland Scottish V883S. In December 1985 Highland along with Central Scottish took over the running of parts of Newton's Travel (Dingwall) operations. Highland inherited a number of vehicles too and at the time it was agreed to continue to use the Newton's name and livery. V883S is pictured at Perth bus station in Newton's travel livery while operating a Scottish Citylink service to Edinburgh. V883S was originally registered A639 EJS and was a Volvo B10M fitted with Van Hool Alizee bodywork.

A183 UGB Highland Scottish
Z893S. Plaxton Paramount
3200-bodied Leyland Tiger Z893S
is pictured at Glasgow Buchanan
bus station. This vehicle and
sister Z882 (A182 UGB) joined
the Highland fleet in 1986 from
Western Scottish and was part of
a large batch that ended up in the
Clydeside, Midland and Lowland
fleets. These vehicles were unusual
in being fitted with Gardner
engines rather than Leyland units.

B875 UST Highland Scottish
E191S. Highland took delivery
of a batch of six Leyland Tigers
fitted with updated Duple Laser II
bodywork in 1985. E191S is
pictured on a private hire duty
outside Inverness Farraline Park
bus station and is wearing the
latest version of the Highland
coach livery at the time, grey with
blue bands.

B871 UST Highland Bus &
Coach E187T. Another member
of the batch, E187T, is again
pictured at Inverness Farraline
Park bus station looking smart
wearing Highland Bus & Coach
all-over-red livery. This vehicle
previously wore Scottish Citylink
livery. The T depot code would
suggest the vehicle is allocated to
Thurso, however it is seen with a
window label for 'Town Centre'.

D154 NON Highland
Scottish P4. Competition
from other operators,
especially Inverness Traction,
prompted Highland to
purchase a small fleet of
minibuses. D154 NON
was one of three Freight
Rover vehicles bodied by
Carlyle that joined the
Highland fleet in 1989 from
Bournemouth. P4 is pictured
in Highland Terrier livery at
the rear of Inverness Seafield
Road depot.

D316 MHS Highland
Scottish Q406S. Alexander
AM-bodied Dodge S56
D316 MHS started life with
Central Scottish in 1986.
She was part of a batch
of seven that joined the
Highland fleet from Kelvin
Central in 1990 and is
pictured in Highland Terrier
livery, departing from
Queensgate Inverness on
service 2B to Culloden via
Raigmore Hospital.

E401 TBS Highland Scottish
Q401S. A later batch of five
Renault S56 minibuses arrived in
1988 fitted with a revised style
of Alexander AM bodywork.
A comparison to the previous
photograph of Q406S shows that
this version of the AM bodywork
features a revised front end and
the side windows fitted higher up.
Overall this gives the impression
of a taller vehicle. Q401S, the
first of the batch, is pictured at
Inverness Farraline Park bus
station working service 4 to
Milton.

B891 UAS Highland Scottish J363S. When this photo was taken, J363S was a long way from its Inverness home. It was actually taken at Fife Scottish Aberhill depot and J363S appears about to enter service on route 61 to Lower Methill. I can find no record of this vehicle passing to Fife permanently so can only assume this was a temporary loan. She is pictured wearing a special version of the red-and-grey livery that many of this batch of vehicles wore. However, it has not been fitted with the eagle garter which many double-deck vehicles in the Highland fleet received on the upper paneling. Sister vehicle B892 UAS has recently entered preservation in this livery complete with the eagle garter and is part of the GVVT collection in Glasgow.

C373 CAS Highland Scottish F373S. A batch of nine Leyland Olympians with Alexander RL bodywork arrived in 1986. Out of the nine vehicles, six were fitted with coach seating and given blue-and-grey coach livery. F373S is one of the coach-seated examples and is pictured in the yard at Aviemore depot. Highland was a big user of the Wayfarer 1 ticket machines as can be seen fitted to F373. This version of the Wayfarer used thermal paper for the tickets and was rather slow at printing tickets. Many SBG companies quickly moved onto the faster Wayfarer II machine.

C380 CAS Highland Bus & Coach J380S. Another member of the 1986 batch of Leyland Olympians is seen in Inverness Farraline Park bus station about to head out east on service 10 to Auldearn. J380 is one of the three vehicles fitted with bus-style seating and is looking smart wearing Highland Bus & Coach red-and-grey livery.

SAS 859T Highland Scottish D317S. Highland operated a number of ECW-bodied Daimler and Leyland Fleetlines. Some, including D317, seen here outside the Post Office in the Queensgate, Inverness, were new to Highland while others arrived from Central and Fife Scottish. D317 is seen operating service 12 to Balloch with a Stagecoach Mercedes 0709 minibus waiting behind. Inverness was another location that saw fierce deregulation competition, mainly with Stagecoach-owned Inverness Traction. After a short 'war' Highland almost withdrew completely from the Inverness services and disposed of many of its more modern vehicles.

OST 255S Highland Scottish T155W. Highland was still operating Ford R1114 vehicles fitted with Alexander AYS bodies as late as 1989. T155W is seen at the Cairngorm ski grounds preparing to work service 38 back to Aviemore. Many of the vehicles used for the Ski-Bus routes wore special liveries, however T155W is pictured wearing standard poppy red and grey livery. The W depot code would suggest this is a vehicle normally allocated to Wick depot, which may explain the paper label in the window.

CAS 513W Highland Scottish L219R. CAS 513W was part of a batch of ten Alexander AY-bodied Leyland Leopards delivered to Highland Scottish in 1981. They were all fitted with forty-nine dual-purpose seats. When Oban depot passed to Midland Scottish in 1985, two members of the batch, CAS 519W and CAS 520W, passed to Midland. Over time both CAS 519W and CAS 520W would enter preservation. CAS 513W was still recorded in service as late as October 2004, working for 2travel in Llanelli, Wales. However, it was ultimately scrapped at a later date.

XSG 69R Highland Scottish L869A. Leyland Leopard L869A, fitted with fifty-three-seat Alexander AYS bodywork, joined the Highland fleet from Midland Scottish in 1988. She is pictured still wearing her Midland livery with Highland fleet names in the yard at Aviemore depot. The paper label in the windscreen reads 'Ski Ground/Aviemore' which would suggest the vehicle has just finished working a service from the Cairngorms ski ground.

ULS 629X Kelvin Scottish 1627. The first livery introduced by Kelvin was a rather dull azure and light blue livery. This was quickly changed to a two-tone blue-and-yellow livery. The fleet was renumbered in the summer of 1986 in an unusual system with the first number representing the type of vehicle. 1 being a bus, 2 a dual-purpose vehicle, 3 would be for coaches and 4 for Citylink-liveried vehicles. 1627 is pictured in Glasgow Buchanan bus station wearing original two-tone blue livery complete with 'Hop On' logos.

LMS 161W Kelvin Scottish 1533. Kelvin's second livery was much brighter and featured a large area of yellow paint. Alexander AD-bodied Leyland Fleetline 1533 is pictured in Glasgow Anderston bus station. The bus station is long gone and finally closed completely in 1993. The area above the former bus station now forms part of Cadogan Square. Kelvin fitted many of its vehicles with destination blinds printed with yellow writing on blue background, as can be seen with 1533. LMS 161W would later pass to Western Scottish in 1989.

D679 MHS Kelvin Scottish 2679. Kelvin took delivery in 1986 of a batch of ten Alexander RL-bodied MCW Metrobuses, all fitted with dual-purpose style seating. All were used on express services between Glasgow and Cumbernauld and wore a revised reversed version of the livery which was designed to give the impression of a fast express service. These were lovely machines to travel on and regrettably none survived into preservation. 2679 is pictured at Glasgow Green taking part in a promotional event with other vehicles from SBG companies.

BLS 431Y Kelvin Scottish 1640. The next version of the Kelvin livery featured the same colours as before but applied in a simpler style. 1640 is pictured in Glasgow Anderston bus station and has been additionally fitted with Cumbernauld's Buses on the lower panels.

C803 KHS Kelvin Scottish 2813. 2813 was part of a batch of ten Leyland Olympians fitted with Alexander RL bodywork delivered to Central Scottish in 1986. They were originally used on Central Redline express services to East Kilbride (C810 KHS featured earlier in this book in Central Redline livery). All ten vehicles were later transferred to the KirkieBus fleet and received this revised Kelvin livery. 2813 is pictured next to a Clydeside Scottish Leyland Leopard in Glasgow Buchanan bus station.

10 CLT Kelvin Scottish RM1010. Kelvin built up a large fleet of ex-London Transport Routemasters. RM1010 is pictured at Glasgow Green in full Kelvin livery taking part in a promotional event with vehicles from other SBG companies. RM1010 would also receive fleet number 1933 during its stay with Kelvin. In 1993 RM1010 moved to Manchester and was converted to open-top in 1996. She returned back north of the border in 2001 and operated on the City tour in Edinburgh. In 2010 she migrated to Virginia, USA, and was used to convey passengers to the Military Aviation museum.

EDS 107A Kelvin Central 1935. Like other operators of the ex-London Transport Routemasters, Kelvin began to remove the original Routemaster number plates. 1935 was originally RM1053, registered 53 CLT, and is pictured wearing Kelvin Central red-and-cream livery in Glasgow Anderston bus station. Route 5 was a regular route for Kelvin's Routemasters and operated between Easterhouse to the east of Glasgow through the city and on to Old Kilpatrick or Faifley in the west. Virtually all of the route would compete with Strathclyde's Buses. 1935 was later reregistered YVS 287 and operated in a green-and-cream livery for Routemaster Bournemouth.

YFS 305W Kelvin Scottish 1275. Kelvin acquired a number of Leyland Nationals from other SBG companies. YFS 305W was new to Eastern Scottish as N305. It then passed to Central Scottish as N66. Later YFS 305W would pass to CMS Carlislebus and was recorded scrapped in 1990. 1275 is pictured heading east on Cathedral Street, Glasgow, passing over Glasgow's Queen Street station. This location has changed dramatically over the years and is now dominated by the Glasgow Royal Concert Hall and Buchanan Galleries shopping complex.

FGG 603X Kelvin Central 2306. Kelvin inherited a number of Alexander T-bodied Leyland Tigers from Central Scottish. 2306 was originally number LT3 with Central and is seen outside Cumbernauld depot, painted in the second version of Kelvin livery.

THN 261F Kelvin Scottish 0998. Kelvin acquired four half-cab vehicles to use in their training fleet. 0998 is a Bristol FLF built in 1968 and fitted with ECW bodywork. It was originally no. 561 in the United Automobile fleet and also operated as 2872 with Northern General. It later passed to Western Scottish as W7059 before passing to Kelvin. 0998 is pictured leaving the main shed at Old Kilpatrick depot with another member of the training fleet, 0996, in the background. 0996 (OFS 777) was a Metro Cammell-bodied Leyland Titan formerly with Lothian Regional Transport and now happily preserved in the collection at SVBM, Lathalmond.

PSF 315Y Lowland Scottish 315. When Lowland was formed it had just over 100 vehicles in the fleet, making it the smallest SBG company. All but nine vehicles were received from the Eastern Scottish fleet. Alexander T-bodied Leyland Tiger 315 is pictured in Edinburgh St Andrews Square bus station and is wearing the company's striking malachite-and-yellow livery. 315 has also been fitted with 'Best Bus in the Country' lettering and still proudly wears her Tiger head badge.

A324 BSC Lowland Scottish 324. Lowland operated the service 95 Scottish Borders Rail Link. This service operated from Edinburgh via Galashields and Hawick to Carlisle, where 324 is pictured. This service was to replace trains on the Edinburgh and Carlisle 'Waverley Route' which closed in January 1969. The line later reopened in 2015 between Edinburgh and Tweedbank. 324 is pictured wearing advertising for the Scottish Borders Rail Link.

J301 ASH Lowland 301. In 1991 Lowland received a batch of four Leyland Tigers fitted with unusual forty-nine-seat dual-purpose Alexander (Belfast) Q bodies. These were among the last Leyland Tigers built. 301, the first of the batch, is seen outside Edinburgh St Andrews Square bus station getting ready to depart on service 95 to Hawick.

DFS 795S Lowland Scottish 495. Something makes me think that this Plaxton Supreme III-bodied Seddon Pennine VII does not want to do any more work today! She is pictured at Edinburgh St Andrews Square bus station with inspector and driver attempting to gain access to the vehicle. The Lowland livery suited these vehicles well.

G715 OSH Lowland 715. Lowland was responsible for operating the Border Courier network of services and used a small fleet of Reeve Burgess-bodied Bedford VAS5 vehicles. These vehicles allowed the carriage of goods for the Borders Health Board and Regional/District council as well as fare-paying passengers. 715 was a later Leyland Swift vehicle fitted with a Reeve Burgess Harrier body delivered in 1989. She is pictured in fleet livery complete with Border Courier logos attending the Dunbar vintage vehicle rally.

ULS 675T Midland Scottish MRF150. Midland operated a number of Daimler and Leyland Fleetlines fitted with either ECW, Alexander or Northern Counties bodywork. ECW-bodied example MRF150 is pictured resting at Falkirk bus station.

LMS 166W Midland Scottish MRF166. The highest numbered Fleetline in the fleet, MRF166 is one of a number fitted with Alexander's AD bodywork and is pictured on layover at Falkirk bus station.

ULS 637X Midland Scottish MRM37. After production of the Fleetline finished, Midland standardised on the MCW Metrobus fitted with Alexander RL bodywork. Upon the 1985 reorganisation Midland lost eighty-one of its 107 Metrobuses, mostly to Kelvin Scottish. MRM37, one of the vehicles remaining in the fleet, is pictured at Falkirk bus station complete with 'Best Bus in Town' lettering.

E771 PSG Midland Scottish RM818. RM818 was an Alexander RL-bodied MCW Metrobus fitted with dual-purpose style seating, part of a batch of five delivered in 1987. She was delivered with registration E618 NLS, but later received a cherished number FSU 309 before finally becoming E771 PSG. RM818 is pictured in Stirling bus station and has been fitted with a rather large Bluebird fleet name and logo.

ALS 105Y Midland Scottish MPT105. Grangemouth-based Alexander T-bodied Leyland Tiger MPT105 dates from 1983 and is fitted with forty-nine dual-purpose seats. It is pictured in Falkirk bus station and wears a version of the livery often fitted with Midland Coaches fleet names.

RMS 398W Midland Bluebird B 398. This Alexander T-bodied vehicle was on a Leyland Leopard chassis and was again fitted with forty-nine dual-purpose seats. 398 was allocated to Balfron depot, which still exists today as a FirstGroup depot. She is pictured at Stirling bus station getting ready to head back to Glasgow via Balfron, wearing a version of Midland Bluebird livery introduced after GRT purchased the company in September 1990.

ULS 338T Midland Scottish PE338. Some of Midland's Alexander Y Type Leyland Leopards received dual-purpose seats cascaded from dual-purpose vehicles which had been upgraded to coach seats. They received a modified livery with a greater amount of cream. PE338 was not one of the chosen ones and remained in standard bus livery complete with fifty-three bus seats. In 1989 the M prefix was removed from fleet numbers, as can be seen with PE338 pictured on layover at Stirling bus station.

OPV 239 Midland Scottish PT123. OPV 239 was originally registered A123 ESG and was a Leyland Tiger from 1984 fitted with a Duple Caribbean body. Midland received ten Duple-bodied Leyland Tigers in 1984. Four were fitted with Caribbean bodies, the other six received Laser bodies. When Midland was split in 1985 four Laser-bodied Tigers passed to Kelvin and Strathtay, leaving Midland with just two of the batch. PT123 was fitted with forty-four coach seats and a toilet and is pictured wearing Scottish Citylink livery at Stirling bus station, getting ready to depart to Edinburgh on service X20. PT123 had left the fleet by 1994.

D650 GLS Midland Scottish MM650. Midland received a batch of four twenty-five-seat MCW MetroRiders in 1987. Originally allocated to Alloa, they later moved to Linlithgow. MM650, the last of the batch, is seen at Inchinnan depot in September 1988 taking part in a Clydeside Scottish open day event.

H975 RSG Midland Bluebird Bn 635. Midland increased its fleet of minibuses, taking a few different types over the years. This included Elme Orion-bodied Freight Rover Sherpas, MCW MetroRiders, and Mercedes L608 and 709D fitted with Alexander AM or Reeve Burgess bodywork. Bn 635 was allocated to Bannockburn depot and was part of a batch of ten Alexander AM-bodied Mercedes-Benz 709D vehicles delivered in 1991.

A203 FSA Northern Scottish NCM3. Northern received two MCW Metroliner coaches in 1984. Fitted with MCW bodies seating forty-eighty with a toilet, these rather square-looking coaches received Scottish Citylink livery. NCM3 is pictured at Glasgow Buchanan bus station working Citylink service 548 to Manchester.

A419 FSA Northern Scottish NRT19. In 1984 Northern also received a pair of Leyland Royal Tiger vehicles fitted with Roe Doyen bodywork. These smart looking vehicles seated forty-six, again with an onboard toilet. Originally these vehicles wore Scottish blue-and-white livery, however NRT19 is pictured here wearing Scottish Citylink livery complete with large-style fleet names at Glasgow Buchanan bus station having arrived on Citylink service 965.

C511 SSO Northern Scottish NCM11. Northern operated a fleet of seven MCW Hi-Liner vehicles bodied by MCW. These coaches were similar in appearance to the earlier Leyland Royal Tiger vehicles fitted with Roe Doyen bodywork. They seated forty-eight with an onboard toilet and often worked the joint Citylink National Express Rapide service 806 from Aberdeen to Plymouth. This service was at the time the longest coach service in Britain. NCM11 is pictured at Plymouth Bretonside coach station getting ready to depart on the long journey north to Aberdeen and is pictured wearing Northern's own coach livery with lettering for Citylink Rapide duties. Bretonside coach station closed in September 2016 to be redeveloped into a new leisure complex.

TSV 718 Bluebird Northern CT28. TSV 718 was originally registered B328 LSA and was the first of a batch of five Alexander TC-bodied Leyland Tigers delivered in 1985 that seated forty-seven. Northern started to use the Bluebird Northern name in spring 1989, but in March 1991 ownership of the company passed to Stagecoach. CT28 was later numbered 442 and is pictured in Aberdeen's Guild Street bus station, freshly repainted into Stagecoach stripes complete with Bluebird Northern fleet names.

RLS 465T Strathtay Scottish SF17. Strathtay operated a total of twenty-two Ford vehicles, being a mix of R1014 and R1114 types. All joined the Strathtay fleet from either Midland or Northern upon the formation of Strathtay in 1985. SF17 was fitted with an Alexander AYS body seating forty-five and is pictured at Crieff depot wearing the revised version of the bus livery with the addition of white to the French blue and marigold colours. SF17 left the fleet in October 1987 and was recorded as scrapped in 1991. Crieff depot and bus station closed in August 1991 and the premises are now used as a supermarket.

A113 ESA Strathtay Buses SBT2. In 1987 four Alexander P-bodied Leyland Tigers joined the fleet from Northern Scottish in exchange for Leyland Nationals. All four seated fifty-two and were allocated to Perth depot. SBT2 is pictured heading through Perth on service 5 to Moncreiffe. It is recorded leaving the fleet in 2004.

ORU 738 Strathtay Coaches SL19. SL19 was a forty-nine-seat Duple Dominant Express-bodied Leyland Leopard that joined the Strathtay fleet from Northern Scottish on formation of the company. It was originally registered RRS 45R and later in life also carried RSL 459R. It is pictured inside Crieff depot and is wearing Strathtay Coaches livery. SL19 left the fleet in 1993.

YSF 87S Strathtay Scottish SL60. SL60 is an Alexander AYS-bodied Leyland Leopard that joined the Strathtay fleet in 1987 from Fife Scottish. She is pictured on layover at Perth bus station in the later Strathtay livery that featured the addition of white. SL60 left the fleet as late as 2006 and is now preserved in this livery carrying Stagecoach fleet number 25787. She was recorded visiting SVBM, Lathalmond, in August 2016.

FSU 309 Strathtay Coaches ST8. ST8 was a 1984 Duple Laser-bodied Leyland Tiger, one of a pair that joined the fleet upon formation in 1985 from Midland Scottish. She was originally registered A126 ESG before receiving VLT 42, A651 XGG and finally FSU 309. ST8 is recorded leaving the fleet in 2000 and is pictured here wearing Strathtay Coaches livery in Dundee bus station.

821 DYE Strathtay Coaches ST17. Leyland Tiger ST17 started life in 1981 with a Duple Dominant IV body that seated forty-six with an onboard toilet. Originally new to Eastern Scottish as BSG 546W carrying fleet number XCL546, she later passed to Kelvin Scottish in 1985 as T129X. In 1986 she joined the Strathtay fleet and received registration number 17 CLT shortly after. She then carried XDS 685W before finally receiving 821 DYE. In May 1992 she was one of two vehicles to receive a new fifty-five-seat dual-purpose East Lancs EL2000 body. ST17 is pictured getting ready to depart Dundee bus station on service 20 to Kirriemuir. ST17 is recorded leaving the fleet in 2006, scrapped at RGC Recyclers, Dundee.

G894 FJW Strathtay Buses SS11. Strathtay took delivery of thirteen Renault S56 minibuses with twenty-five-seat Dormobile Routemaker bodywork in 1989. The vehicles were authorised at a time that the SBG had halted the purchase of any new vehicles. The vehicles were purchased from dealer stock and were required to compete against Stagecoach in Perth, who had deployed a fleet of Panther Cub minibuses. The fleet initially operated in a red-and-cream livery; Perth City Transport with City Nipper lettering. SS11 later acquired Strathtay livery and was recorded as scrapped in June 1998. SS11 is pictured at Dundee bus station having arrived on route 77A. I wonder if the big red button on the front activates the Turbo!

WTS 101A Strathtay Bus & Coach SR12. Strathtay borrowed two Routemaster vehicles from Clydeside Scottish in November 1985 and as a result an initial batch of twenty were purchased for delivery with a few more arriving at a later date. The Routemasters operated in both Perth and Dundee where Strathtay was experiencing competition after deregulation. They initially operated in an unusual striped version of the livery, with some also acquiring a red-and-cream livery with Perth City Transport lettering. Later arrivals received fleet livery applied in a more conventional style and SR12 is seen here in Dundee bus station, also having been repainted into this style. Originally registered VLT 183, she received WTS 101A in 1988 with her original Routemaster registration transferring to Leyland Tiger coach ST6. Note the destination screen above the rear platform has been painted out. Strathtay's Routemasters remained in service longer than both the Clydeside and Kelvin Scottish fleets.

ASA 25T Strathtay Scottish SD14. Upon formation in 1985 Strathtay received sixteen Daimler and Leyland Fleetlines from both Midland Scottish and Northern Scottish fleets. Some were fitted with Alexander bodies with the rest being ECW-bodied, as seen on SD14 pictured inside Crieff depot. This was the original Strathtay livery before the addition of the white stripe. I always preferred the bold colours of the livery without the white, but many felt it was rather dark and the white helped to brighten it up. SD14 was one of the Fleetlines to join the fleet from Northern Scottish and was later re-registered AES 116T.

LMS 156W Strathtay Scottish SD15. Representing one of the Alexander-bodied Fleetlines, SD15 is pictured working service 1 in Perth and joined the Strathtay fleet from Midland Scottish. She is pictured again wearing the original version of the livery complete with 'Best Bus Around' lettering. SD15 later received registration WGB 711W and reportedly survives on a farm near Errol.

D819 EES Strathtay Scottish SO19. A small batch of three Alexander RL-bodied Leyland Olympians joined the Strathtay fleet in 1987. SO19 was the final member of the batch and is pictured outside Edinburgh St Andrew Square bus station on a sunny day. SO19 was later preserved in Strathtay Coaches livery.

KKY 833P Strathtay Buses SB6. Ownership of Strathtay passed to the Yorkshire Traction group in June 1991. A few months later a batch of seven Bristol VRTs with ECW bodywork joined the fleet – an unusual vehicle for a Scottish operator. They were painted at Barnsley before heading north. SB6 is pictured outside Dundee Seagate depot next to the Dundee bus station. The depot closed in August 2008 when Strathtay relocated to bigger premises at Wester Gourdie industrial estate. In August 2016 this depot also closed, leaving Strathtay with no depot in Dundee.

YSD 817T Western Scottish KS 517. Until 1985 the majority of the bus fleet was painted in a red-and-cream livery, as worn by KS 517. She was an Alexander AY-bodied Seddon Pennine VII from 1978, pictured here in the yard at Kilmarnock depot. The C8 above the fleet number on the side indicates the vehicle is from 1978.

TSJ 86S Western Scottish AL 686. The next livery introduced by Western in 1985 was a black-and-white livery with grey bands, as seen here on AL 686. She is pictured in the yard at the company's Ayr depot and is an Alexander AY-bodied Leyland Leopard new in 1977. This was a very common vehicle type in the Western fleet and in this photo the previous red-and-cream livery is beginning to show through.

GCS 37V Western Scottish AL737. The next version of the livery reduced the amount of grey and introduced some red. It was much brighter than the last livery and suited most vehicles well. AL 737 was an Alexander AY-bodied Leyland Leopard, part of a batch of forty delivered to Western in 1980, and would be the final Alexander AY-bodied Leyland Leopards delivered to Western. AL 737 was unusual, being fitted with dual-purpose seating, and is pictured in Glasgow Buchanan bus station getting ready to depart to New Cumnock on express service 501. The author has preserved similar GCS 50V in red-and-yellow Clydeside Scottish livery.

MSJ 370P Western Scottish KS 564. KS 564 was an Alexander T-bodied Seddon Pennine VII from 1976. Western converted four of the batch to seat twenty-four and accommodate wheelchairs with a side-mounted lift. Of the four, three passed to Central and Midland Scottish with Western retaining KS 564. She is pictured in the original black, white and grey livery worn by dual-purpose vehicles at a promotional event at Glasgow Green. Sister vehicle MSJ 385P also fitted with a wheelchair lift joined the Central Scottish fleet in 1984 and lives on in preservation as part of the GVVT collection in Glasgow retaining her converted layout.

DSD 937V Western Scottish KS 437. KS 437, a later Alexander T-bodied Seddon Pennine VII from 1980, is pictured in the yard at Kilmarnock depot wearing the later Western dual-purpose livery. This view also shows she has received a smaller single-piece rear window at some point, which was a modification carried out by SBG to many of their T Type vehicles.

703 DYE Western CN 403. CN 403 was originally registered TSD 153Y and was a Dennis Dorchester fitted with a Plaxton Paramount 3200 body seating forty-nine. It was part of a trial batch of eight vehicles purchased in 1983 alongside Volvo B10M vehicles fitted with Duple bodywork. The batch was received wearing a revised version of the dual-purpose livery designed by Plaxtons for the Paramount bodywork complete with Cityliner lettering. Most of the batch passed to Clydeside Scottish upon formation of the company. However, CN 403 remained with Western. CN 403 is pictured at Cumnock depot and by the time the picture was taken has been fitted with the registration number 703 DYE from Routemaster RM1703 and is wearing the later version of the Western coach livery.

D221 NCS Western Scottish DN 221. Western ordered a second batch of six Dennis Dorchester vehicles in 1987, this time fitted with fifty-five-seat Alexander TC bodies. Four of the batch wore Scottish Citylink livery. However, DN 221 was one of a pair painted in black, white and grey dual-purpose livery and is pictured in Edinburgh St Andrews Square bus station.

WLT 720 Western SV 198. Western took delivery of an unusual Berkhof Esprit-bodied Volvo B10M vehicle in 1985. Originally registered B198 CGA, she received WLT 720 from Routemaster RM720 and is pictured outside Stranraer depot during an organised visit for the Western Enthusiast Club.

C206 HSD Western LH 106.
In 1986 Western received three Hestair-Duple 425 vehicles seating fifty-four with a toilet also fitted. These smart vehicles were often used on London services. Originally painted in Scottish Citylink livery, LH 106 is pictured wearing later Western coach livery in the yard of Thornliebank depot. The late well-respected transport photographer Robert Grieves is pictured at the wheel.

MDS 858V Western AL 778.
A surprise purchase for Western in 1988 was a batch of twenty Leyland Nationals from Kelvin Scottish. AL 778 was new to Central Scottish in 1980 and passed to Kelvin Scottish in 1986. AL 778 is pictured inside Ayr depot and has been painted in an unusual version of the livery with grey in place of black and black in place of grey. She also retains yellow on blue number blinds from her Kelvin days.

D239 NCS Western Scottish AD 239. The first batch of minibuses ordered by Western was a batch of forty Alexander AM-bodied Dodge S56s, a popular combination with many SBG companies. The batch was deployed on services around Ayr and Prestwick and carried a revised livery with 'Ayr Buzzers' logos fitted. AD 239 is pictured in Ayr town centre, heading to Moorfield on service 6.

D118 NUS Western Scottish KZ 218. Western acquired a batch of twenty-four Alexander AM-bodied Mercedes L608 minibuses from Kelvin Scottish in 1987 at a time when Kelvin was reducing its fleet due to financial difficulties. This batch of minibuses seated twenty-one and KZ 218 is pictured at Ardrossan depot, a sub-depot of Kilmarnock, wearing a later version of Western's 'Buzzers' livery.

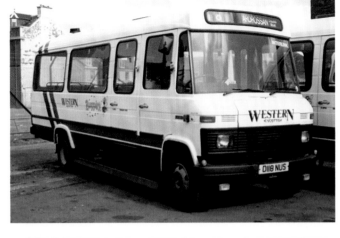

G832 VGA Western MT 279. Between 1989 and 1990 Western took delivery of a number of unusual Tri Axle Talbot Pullman minibuses fitted with twelve-seat Talbot bodies. The vehicles were used for Dial-A-Bus services throughout Strathclyde region and the vehicles were fitted with a tail lift for wheelchairs. A number of the vehicles passed to Clydeside including MT 279, pictured here with a number of sister vehicles inside Thornliebank depot.

B924 BGA Scottish Citylink LV 211. LV 211 was one of a pair of sixty-four-seat Plaxton Paramount 4000-bodied Volvo B10M vehicles that joined the Western fleet in 1985 from the Newton's of Dingwall fleet. Although carrying Western fleet names and numbers, LV 211 was actually owned by Scottish Citylink and maintained by Western. She is pictured wearing Scottish Citylink livery on layover at Warroch Street, Glasgow, a yard later used by Stagecoach for its Glasgow Magicbus operations.

A161 TGE Western Scottish
LM 161. LM161 was one
of three sixty-nine-seat
MCW-bodied MCW Metroliner
coaches delivered to Western in
1984. LM161 is pictured wearing
Scottish Citylink livery at the
company's Kilmarnock depot.
Sister vehicle LM162 can be
seen in the background wearing
a slightly different version of
the livery complete with MCW
badge. Three similar vehicles
joined the Western fleet in 1989
from Northern Scottish.

B187 CGA Western Scottish LV
187. After acquiring a former
demonstrator vehicle from Ensign
dealers in 1985, Western went on
to order a pair of similar Berkhof
Emperor fifty-six-seat-bodied
Volvo B10M vehicles in 1985.
They were the last vehicles in the
fleet to wear the blue-and-white
Scottish livery. LV 187 is pictured
at a motorway service station on
route to London.

GOG 566N Western Scottish
CR 809. A rather unusual batch
of vehicles to join the fleet in
1987 were ten Park Royal-bodied
Daimler Fleetlines new to West
Midland's PTE in 1973 and 1975.
Wearing Cumnock depot codes,
CR 809 is pictured at Largs depot
in black, white and grey livery.

UNA 772S Western DA 807. Western also acquired a small number of Leyland Atlanteans from GM Buses in 1991 with either Park Royal or Northern Counties bodies. These vehicles were at first on loan to Western and received temporary fleet numbers. DA 807 is pictured in the yard at Dumfries depot, still wearing GM Buses livery complete with Western fleet names.

KUC 915P Western Scottish NR 823. Another batch of second-hand Fleetlines operated by Western were MCW-bodied DMS Fleetlines acquired in 1983 from London Transport. Some of the batch passed to Clydeside Scottish, leaving seventeen with Western. NR 823 is pictured in the yard at Ardrossan depot wearing the later version of the livery.

ECS 876V Western CR 876. Northern Counties-bodied Leyland Fleetline CR 876 is pictured at Western's Cumnock depot. Although new to Western she passed to Clydeside Scottish in 1985 upon the formation of the company and was based at Thornliebank depot. She rejoined the Western fleet in 1988 and is pictured in the final version of the Western livery prior to the Stagecoach takeover.

ULS 657T Western JR 357. JR 357, an ECW-bodied Leyland Fleetline, was part of a batch of Leyland Fleetlines fitted with both Alexander AD and ECW bodies that joined the fleet from Kelvin Scottish. New to Midland Scottish in 1979, these vehicles were acquired by Western in 1989 to boost the fleet and assist with the removal of the crew-operated Routemasters. JR 357 is pictured at Inchinnan depot.

C155 FDS Western JN 955. A later photograph of C155 FDS, one of a batch of five Alexander RL-bodied Dennis Dominator vehicles, this time pictured at Johnstone depot. She was new to Clydeside Scottish and received Clydeside Quicksilver livery, as seen on page 17, after being fitted with dual-purpose seats. Seen here still fitted with her dual-purpose seats, JN 955 is pictured in the final version of Western livery. The thin white stripe between decks was actually white sticky tape!

A729 YFS Lothian LRT 729. The first two Olympians delivered to Lothian had Alexander bodies. However, for the rest of the deliveries over the next few years Lothian opted for 10.2-m ECW bodies seating eighty-one. These bodies were longer than normal and had an extra short bay fitted. 729 is seen heading along Princes Street, Edinburgh, operating service 3 to Mayfield.

E307 MSG Lothian LRT 307. After the demise of ECW, Lothian returned to Alexander's and a batch of thirty-six long-length Olympians, again seating eighty-one, were delivered in 1988 with Alexander RH bodywork. 307 is seen heading along Edinburgh's Princes Street, passing the famous Jenners department store. An Eastern Scottish Volvo Ailsa can be seen in the background. Later in life this vehicle was converted to part open-top and operated the Citysightseeing tour in Edinburgh before moving on and again operating the Citysightseeing tour with Transdev in York.

GFS 429N Lothian LRT 429. Before the Leyland Olympian, Lothian opted for the Leyland Atlantean with seventy-five-seat Alexander AL bodywork. Representing a batch of sixty-four vehicles delivered in 1975, 429 is pictured in Edinburgh working service 2, which would appear to be a Circle. The AL body could be specified with large panoramic windows, as seen on 429.

J840 TSC Lothian LRT 840. Leyland Olympian 840 was fitted with Alexander RH bodywork. Again this batch was fitted with an eighty-one-seat longer body. As can be seen in this picture of 840 taken in St Andrews Square, Edinburgh, the extra length is achieved by adding an extra short bay window mid-body. Vehicles delivered after 1990 including 840 were fitted with marker lights on the roof.

HDV 639E Stagecoach PS2. Stagecoach was formed in 1980 to take advantage of the deregulation of express coach services in 1980. The company then went on in April 1986 to expand in both Perth and Glasgow. Stagecoach has continued to grow and is now the largest bus operator in the UK, eventually owning five members of the Scottish Bus Group companies. The first vehicle to join the fleet was HDV 639E, a Bristol MW6G from 1967 fitted with ECW bodywork. She joined Stagecoach from the Western National fleet and is pictured wearing Stagecoach stripes livery during an open day at SVBM, Whitburn. Happily, HDV 639E lives on and is now part of the SVBM collection at Lathalmond, wearing Midland Bluebird livery.

602 DYE Magicbus. Stagecoach registered new services from Glasgow to East Kilbride, Castlemilk and Easterhouse from deregulation day in October 1986. The company used the Magicbus name along with standard Stagecoach livery. The East Kilbride service was dropped quickly but the other two services remained. A mixed fleet was operated from ex-London Transport Routemasters to new Mercedes minibuses. 602 DYE, former London Transport RM1602, is pictured in the company of another ex-London Routemaster at Dixon Street, Glasgow, getting ready to depart on service 20 to Castlemilk. Magicbus was not permitted to use the bus station located across the road at St Enoch's Square as this was owned by Strathclyde's Buses.

MAU 142P Stagecoach 093. In 1991 Stagecoach took a batch of ECW-bodied Bristol VRT vehicles from East Midlands. 093 was new in 1976 and is pictured on a very wet day, again at the Dixon Street terminus, loading for Castlemilk on service 20. 093 eventually headed back down south, joining the NIBS Buses fleet in Wickford, Essex.

G298 TSL Magicbus. Stagecoach placed an order for 100 Mercedes 709D minibuses fitted with Alexander AM twenty-five-seat bodywork, which arrived in 1990. The vehicles were distributed around many of the Stagecoach fleets and transfers were common. A nearly-new example, G298 TSL, is pictured in Dixon Street, Glasgow, uplifting passengers for service 20 to Castlemilk. The completed St Enoch's Shopping Centre can be seen in the background. During this time your author worked at the Polmadie train depot in the south side of Glasgow and made a point of using this service regularly – never knowing if it was going to be a Routemaster, Bristol VRT or Mercedes minibus! G298 TSL was last spotted in November 2016 being broken up for spares after operating as a Cocktail on Wheels private hire vehicle!

2412 SC Stagecoach. New to Stagecoach in 1985 was this Auwaerter Neoplan Jetliner coach seating fifty-three with an onboard toilet. Originally registered B683 DVL, she is pictured at Edinburgh's St Andrews Square bus station on another very wet day. By 1990 she carried registration B660 XTS and wore Caledonian Express livery. The coach would eventually pass to Ringwood of Chesterfield.

F110 NES Magicbus 1. When delivered in April 1989, F110 NES was Britain's biggest bus, seating 110; hence the registration number carried. A Tri Axle Leyland Olympian fitted with Alexander RL bodywork featuring three-and-two seating, she was normally found working Magicbus services in the Glasgow area or school services. She is pictured visiting the SVBM at Whitburn during an open day event. She quickly moved on from Magicbus to United Counties, Bedford, and is now semi-preserved, destined to join the SVBM collection at Lathalmond.

KGG143Y Strathclyde's Buses LO 23. Leyland Olympian LO 23 is pictured in Glasgow's George Square taking part in a promotional exercise. She has been fitted with a removable smiling front. She was delivered to Strathclyde in 1983 and is part of a batch of twenty-four Olympians delivered that year fitted with ECW bodywork. She ended her days with First Edinburgh at Dalkeith depot.

GGE 175T Strathclyde's Buses LN 20. Greater Glasgow PTE took delivery of a batch of twenty Leyland Nationals in 1979 including LN 20. LN 20 is one of a pair sent when new direct from Leyland to Islay to help out after a local operator ceased trading. The entire batch had left the Strathclyde fleet by 1988 with the exception of LN 20, the last in the batch, which was converted to a publicity vehicle. She is pictured at an open day event at SVBM Whitburn and is looking very happy to be there!

XUS 573S Strathclyde's Buses LA 1202. Glasgow was a big user of the Leyland Atlantean, ordering them right up to 1981 when LA 1449 was delivered. All were fitted with Alexander AL bodywork. However, some were dual-door and some had panoramic windows. LA 1202 was part of a batch of sixty-six delivered in 1977 with panoramic windows and seventy-eight-seat Alexander AL bodywork. She is pictured turning into Stockwell Street from Osborne Street, Glasgow, while working service 62 to Airdrie. A large Argos store now occupies the space behind the bus.

HGD 916L Strathclyde's Buses LA 710. This Alexander-bodied Leyland Atlantean LA 710 was part of a batch delivered in 1972 with short bay windows. It was originally a dual-door vehicle and by the time this picture was taken she had been converted to a training vehicle. The vehicle features an interesting conversion and appears to have lost both doors!

KGG 132Y Strathclyde's Buses A 72. After the last Leyland Atlantean was delivered in 1981, Strathclyde PTE ordered a mix of MCW Metrobuses, Leyland Olympians and Volvo Ailsas. A 72 was an Alexander RV-bodied Volvo Ailsa MK III, part of a batch of 116 delivered between 1981 and 1983. She is pictured in the yard at Larkfield depot. The depot experienced a serious fire in 1992 when almost sixty buses were destroyed. Larkfield depot closed in October 2014 after eighty-five years of operation.

A603 TNS Strathclyde's Buses AH 4. At first glance AH 4 might look just like another Volvo Ailsa with Alexander RV bodywork, but it is actually a Volvo Citybus. She was part of a batch of five delivered in 1983 suitable for the carriage of six wheelchairs by fitting a hydraulic lift within the normal entrance and six tip-up seats in the lower deck. Her lower deck seating capacity was reduced to twenty-seven. The hydraulic lift can be seen in this photograph, taken in the yard at Parkhead depot during a rather wet open day event.

ESU 378X Strathclyde's Buses AH 1. The first Volvo Citybus to join the Strathclyde PTE fleet was AH 1, built in 1982. She was the prototype Volvo Citybus and was fitted with Marshall bodywork seating eighty-six. Strathclyde PTE also took two similar Marshall-bodied Volvo Ailsas in 1984. AH 1 is pictured in the yard at Larkfield depot complete with Volvo Ailsa badge on the front grill! Many people think AH1 was lost in the Larkfield fire. It actually received rear end damage but was repaired and survived until 1998.

G688 PNS Strathclyde's Buses AH 60. Strathclyde's Buses went on to order a further ninety-five Volvo Citybuses, all fitted with a new version of the Alexander RV bodywork seating eighty-four. The Strathclyde vehicles, however, featured a revised front bumper and round headlamps. AH 60 passed to First Manchester and was later exported in 2007 to Malta where she was converted to open-top. In this photograph a newly delivered AH 60 is seen taking part in an open day event at Parkhead depot.

MUS 309Y Strathclyde's Buses MB 31. Strathclyde took five batches of MCW Metrobuses between 1979 and 1989. The batch of twenty-five delivered in 1989 would be the last due to late deliveries from MCW. The second batch, MB 6 to MB 20, had Alexander RH bodies. However the rest, including MB 31, had MCW bodywork. MB 31 is seen in the yard at Possilpark depot and requires a replacement window for the top deck. Possilpark depot closed in 2000.

KGG 164Y Strathclyde's Buses MBC 23. Of the Metrobuses delivered in 1983, five were fitted with dual-purpose seats and wore coach livery. MBC 23 is pictured on private hire duties. She later received standard livery but retained her dual-purpose seats.

J138 FYS Strathclyde's Buses LO 49. Strathclyde received three Leyland Olympians fitted with Leyland bodywork in 1991. The three vehicles were to cover for Volvo Citybuses that required warranty work. Sadly, the first, LO 47, was lost in the Larkfield fire in 1992. LO 49 is pictured at Parkhead depot during an open day event.

SGA 733N Strathclyde's Buses SA 1. After capacity problems with Seddon minibuses used on the inter-station service in Glasgow, Strathclyde PTE converted eight early Alexander-bodied Leyland Atlanteans to single-deck seating either thirty-one or thirty-five. Originally LA 850 when new in 1973, SA 1 is pictured operating inter-station service 98 at Glasgow Queen Street station.

MGE 185P Strathclyde's Buses AS 2. Originally delivered as AV 10 and fitted with a double-deck Alexander AV body, she was converted to single-deck in 1985 after an accident. Seating thirty-eight, she is seen wearing coach livery while working inter-station service 98 at Glasgow Queen St station. She later passed to Black Prince of Morley and was operated by them in the mid-1990s until the Ministry of Transport questioned the paperwork for the vehicle, which apparently still recorded the vehicle as a double-deck bus! The Volvo Ailsa had a lot of weight at the front and bodywork manufactures designed their bodywork with extra strengthening to take account of that. While in service with Black Prince AS 2 developed a noticeable droop forward of the front axle which may also have hastened its demise.

A740 RNS Strathclyde's Buses C 13. Strathclyde PTE operated a small fleet of coaches, mostly for private hire duties. C 13 was a MCW Metroliner coach with forty-nine-seat MCW bodywork, one of two delivered in 1983. They were fitted with wheelchair lifts in the front doorway and had a rare double plug door. C 13 is pictured at a wet Parkhead depot during an open day event with some young passengers testing the wheelchair lift. C13 was destroyed during the Larkfield depot fire in 1992.

F384 FYS Strathclyde's Buses AS 3. AS 3 was one of two Plaxton Derwent-bodied Volvo B10M single-deck vehicles delivered to Strathclyde's Buses in 1988. As delivered they had bus seating for fifty-two passengers and carried bus livery. However, they were later reseated with forty-six dual-purpose seats and painted in coach livery. This enabled them to be used on private hire duties if required. A third Plaxton Derwent joined the fleet in 1990 from Graham's of Paisley. AS 3 is pictured at Parkhead depot in its later guise.

J113 XSX Strathclyde's Buses C 940. J113 XSX is pictured at Larkfield depot in Strathclyde's Buses coach livery. This vehicle, along with sister H912 HRO, were Scania demonstrators with Plaxton Verde bodywork and were on loan to the company after the Larkfield fire of 1992. Vehicles on loan to the company received fleet numbers prefixed by C. C940 went on to join the fleet in 1993 and was allocated fleet number SS2.

E197 BNS Strathclyde's Buses M100. Strathclyde's Buses built up a fleet of seventy-five MCW Metrobuses between 1987 and 1989 to help compete with other operators. Later deliveries like M100 were longer and seated thirty-three passengers. M100 is pictured resting between duties and carries 'Your wee happy bus' logos. M100 later passed to Yorkshire Traction then moved north again to join Strathtay in November 2000. She was withdrawn in 2006 and last photographed in a Dundee scrapyard in June 2006.

MVK 516R Strathclyde's Buses LA 1463. Glasgow's own fleet of Leyland Atlanteans only went to LA 1449. After the Larkfield depot fire in 1992 when sixty vehicles were destroyed, Strathclyde borrowed many vehicles of all shapes and sizes to help them maintain services. Many eventually joined the fleet including LA 1463, an Alexander-bodied Atlantean that started life with Tyne and Wear PTE in 1976. The main differences with Glasgow's own fleet was the nearside staircase and extra-large front fog lamps. LA 1463 is pictured in the yard at Parkhead depot. Parkhead depot closed in January 2016 after operating for ninety-three years.

ANA 211T Strathclyde's Buses C920. This vehicle, a Northern Counties-bodied Leyland Atlantean, was on loan to Strathclyde's Buses after the 1992 Larkfield depot fire and arrived from Western Scottish. New to Greater Manchester Transport in 1978, she passed to Western Scottish in 1991 and is pictured in the yard at Knightswood depot. She is seen wearing Western Scottish livery with Strathclyde's Buses orange applied to the front and rear with temporary fleet number C920. Interestingly she has received a replacement front panel carrying GM Buses livery and fleet number 7861 while with Strathclyde. This belongs to a Park Royal-bodied Leyland Atlantean with the registration UNA 861S.

KSA 195P Strathclyde's Buses C928. Another Leyland Atlantean on loan to Strathclyde's Buses in 1992 was C928 from the Grampian Transport fleet. New in 1976 and originally numbered 195, she is a Leyland Atlantean with Alexander dual-door AL body. While in Glasgow the rear doors were not used. C928 is pictured in the yard at Knightswood depot wearing Grampian livery with Strathclyde orange front and rear. Knightswood depot closed in 2004 after serving Glasgow for seventy-two years.

SSN 238S Strathclyde's Buses C904. Among the first loan vehicles were Alexander AV-bodied Volvo Ailsas from Tayside. C904 was new as 238 to Tayside Regional Council in 1977 and is seen wearing Tayside livery complete with Strathclyde orange front and back at Larkfield depot. Again, only the front doors were used while with Strathclyde.

OTO 567M Strathclyde's Buses LA 1453. Also joining the Strathclyde fleet after the 1992 fire was a batch of seven East Lancs-bodied Leyland Atlanteans new to Nottingham Transport. These vehicles received full-fleet livery and had their dual-door removed. LA 1463 is pictured in the yard at Parkhead depot during a visit by the Western Enthusiast Club.

666 TPJ Tayside Buses 312. Tayside operated a small fleet of coaches. 312 was one of a pair of Volvo B10Ms fitted with an unusual Irizar Pyrennean coach bodywork. New as D312 ETS in 1987 and seating forty-nine with an onboard toilet, she was named *Bonnie Dundee*. This vehicle also carried Caledonian Express livery during her time with Tayside.

WTS 263T Tayside Buses 263. The Volvo Ailsa became the standard Tayside vehicle with the first examples arriving in 1976. By 1989 the entire double-deck fleet comprised Volvo Ailsa and Volvo Citybus vehicles, meaning the fleet contained no rear-engined vehicles. 263 was a Volvo Ailsa fitted with Alexander AV bodywork delivered in 1979. She is pictured operating service 1B to St Mary's in King Street, Dundee.

A77 SSP Tayside Buses 77. As well as Alexander AV-bodied Volvo Ailsas, Tayside operated Ailsas with Northern Counties and East Lancs bodywork. 77 is an example from 1983 fitted with eighty-four-seat East Lancs bodywork and is again photographed in King Street, Dundee – this time operating to Ninewells Hospital.

G102 PES Tayside Buses 102. Tayside took fifteen Alexander RV-bodied Volvo Citybuses in 1989. These featured flat glass screens on both decks, resulting in a thicker pillar between the upper deck windows. 102 had a long operating life, passing to Redline of Preston and then Bubble Travel of Burnley. During her time with Redline she carried registration number YIL 6983, later regaining G102 PES. 102 is pictured operating service 29 to Charleston in King Street, Dundee.

D864 PYS Harte Buses Greenock. Greenock experienced more deregulation competition than most towns of its size. One of the first operators to compete was Harte Buses, who in 1986 took delivery of a rare Optare Citypacer. This minibus was produced by Optare from 1985 till 1992 and was based on the Volkswagen LT55 van. Only around 300 were produced, many going to London Transport. Harte Buses survived longer than most other smaller operators in Greenock, finally ceasing trading in 2012.

WGD 695R Inverclyde Transport Greenock. Inverclyde Transport built up a sizable fleet and competed hard against Clydeside Scottish. The first vehicles to join the fleet were unusual ex-MOD Bedford SB5 vehicles with Marshall bodywork, as seen with WGD 695R pictured in Kilblain Street, Greenock. Inverclyde Transport would go on to operate Leyland Nationals and Leyland Leopards – some arriving from other SBG companies! The company was eventually purchased by Clydeside Buses, who retained some of the vehicles, adding them to the Clydeside fleet.

LSE 444P Viking Coaches Largs. Viking Coaches were based in Largs and initially commenced operation in 1987 with a local service around Largs using a Freight Rover minibus. They also owned LSE 444P, a Bedford YRQ with Duple Dominant bodywork, which normally operated a service from Port Glasgow through Greenock, Largs and onto Kilbirnie. This service only lasted till 1988. The coach was new to Maynes of Buckie in 1975 and is pictured on lay over in Largs on the site now occupied by Morrison's supermarket. The Clydeside Scottish depot can be seen in the background.

GNS 670N Clyde Coast Services Ardrossan. Not far along the coast from Largs is Ardrossan, where Clyde Coast Services were based. They were formed in 1929 as a co-operative with four members, growing to six members, but by 1988 only one member remained. The company operated a route from Saltcoats to Largs but sadly no longer trades. GNS 670N was a Leyland Atlantean with Alexander AL bodywork new to Greater Glasgow PTE in 1975 and is pictured in the depot yard. She arrived at Clyde Coast in 1989 from Smith of Dalmellington, Ayrshire. After her time with Clyde Coast she returned to Glasgow, operating for a time with an independent operator in Clydebank.

GGE 169T Millport Motors Ltd. LN14. A short ferry ride from Largs takes you to the island of Great Cumbrae – better known as Millport, which is the main town on the island. Even Millport experienced competition after deregulation with two operators, Millport Motors Ltd and Cumbrae Coaches, competing on the route on the island between the ferry slipway and Millport town centre. The two companies would eventually merge using the Millport Motors name and livery. LN14, an ex-Greater Glasgow PTE Leyland National new in 1979, is seen wearing Millport Motors livery collecting passengers at the ferry slipway with a Cumbrae Coaches vehicles directly behind.

YNV 205J Cumbrae Coaches Millport. Also pictured at the ferry slipway collecting passengers from the Largs ferry is Cumbrae Coaches YNV 205J. She was a Bristol RELH with ECW bodywork new to United Counties in 1971 as fleet number 205. By late 1988 she had migrated back south and was operating for Delta of Stockton.

F792 DWT Edinburgh Transport ET302. Edinburgh Transport was a trading name of long-established Silver Coach Lines, an operator of high-specification coaches in Edinburgh. Edinburgh transport had a fleet of ten vehicles, mostly Leyland Nationals, though they also purchased two DAF SB220 Optare Delta vehicles – a first in Scotland. Both were ex-demonstrators for DAF or Optare and joined the fleet in 1990, wearing a smart orange-and-blue livery. They competed against both Lothian Transport and Eastern Scottish. The company was purchased by Stevensons of Uttoxeter in 1993, which in turn was purchased by British Bus and finally became part of the Arriva group. After Edinburgh Transport ceased trading ET302 moved to the main Stevensons fleet and was pictured in 1998 operating in Burton-on-Trent wearing Arriva livery.

SAO 413R Inverness Traction 123. Inverness Traction was established in 1988 by a group of staff formerly employed by Highland Scottish and started running a fleet of nearly-new Freight Rover minibuses. The company was later acquired by Stagecoach and in 1991, when Highland Scottish was purchased by Rapson, bitter competition broke out with many staff defecting from Highland Scottish to Inverness Traction. Inverness Traction required more vehicles to compete and received many reserve vehicles from other Stagecoach companies. SAO 413R was a Bristol VRT new in 1977 with ECW bodywork that arrived in Inverness from Cumberland in 1991. She is pictured still wearing NBC livery, complete with Cumberland fleet names, in Inverness bus station getting ready to head to Tain on service 25. This service still operates to this day as service 25. By 1994, SAO 413R had headed south to Lincoln and was operating for Carlton Coaches.

RRM 636X Inverness Traction 206. Also received in 1991 from Cumberland was a batch of ten Leyland Leopards fitted with ECW forty-nine-seat bodywork. They dated from 1982 and 206 is pictured in Inverness bus station, getting ready to work service 16. She is still wearing Cumberland livery, fleet numbers and fleet names, but has received a small Inverness Traction fleet name on the front. This vehicle went on to operate with Nicolsons of Borve (Skye) and by 2005 was owned by the Shetland Aid Trust, carrying humanitarian aid supplies to Albania and Romania.

B192 XJD West Coast Motors. West Coast Motors can trace its routes back to 1920 and has served the Kintyre peninsula ever since. A long-distance service that has operated for many years is service 926 between Glasgow and Campbeltown, where West Coast Motors is based. It runs several times a day and takes just over four hours. B192 XJD, a Plaxton Paramount 3200-bodied Volvo B10M new in 1985 and seating forty-nine, joined the West Coast Motors fleet in 1989 from Telling Golden Miller. She is pictured in Glasgow Buchanan bus station on layover after arrival from Campbeltown.

D181 TSB West Coast Motors. A later Mark III Plaxton Paramount 3200 from 1986 and new to West Coast Motors on a Volvo B10M chassis is again pictured in Glasgow Buchanan bus station. West Coast Motors vehicles did not carry fleet numbers until very recently and were always smartly turned out. Most of West Coast Motor's other Plaxton Paramount coaches seated fifty-seat but this coach seated fifty-seven.

F532 ASB West Coast Motors. F532 ASB was one of a pair of Plaxton Paramount-bodied Volvo B10M coaches that joined the fleet new in 1989, seating fifty-three. It is again pictured resting at Glasgow Buchanan bus station having arrived on Scottish Citylink service 575. She is pictured wearing the standard West Coast Motors two-tone red-and-cream coach livery.

F532 ASB West Coast Motors. A later view of F532 ASB, in almost exactly the same location within Glasgow Buchanan bus station, shows her now wearing a later version of the Scottish Citylink livery. This was the only coach in the fleet carrying Scottish Citylink livery at the time. Since 1986 West Coast Motors jointly operated the Kintyre peninsula express services with Scottish Citylink, but in May 2008 the two companies were in dispute over new contracts. West Coast Motors then launched services to compete with Scottish Citylink, which included a discount on the Glasgow Citysightseeing tour that was also operated by West Coast Motors. The disagreement only lasted a few months and after contracts were agreed with West Coast Motors they began operating Scottish Citylink services again in September 2008. At this time many vehicles received a revised livery of half West Coast Motors and half Scottish Citylink.